Exploring the Book of Daniel

Unsealing the Sealed Book

by N.W. Hutchings

Cover illustration by Phan Sbong

All scripture references are from the King James Version unless otherwise stated

Exploring the Book of Daniel
First Edition, 1990
Copyright © by **Hearthstone Publishing**
Oklahoma City, OK 73101

Printed in the United States of America

Published by:
Hearthstone Publishing
P.O. Box 60
Oklahoma City, OK 73101

Library of Congress Catalog Card Number 89-81567
ISBN 0-9624517-0-3

Table of Contents

Preface

"But thou, O Daniel, shut up the words, and seal the book, even to the time of the end: many shall run to and fro, and knowledge shall be increased" (Dan. 12:4).

Adam could gallop through the Garden of Eden on a horse at 30 m.p.h. Five thousand nine hundred years later, man was still limited to about 30 m.p.h. in travel and communications.

Vaccines for deadly diseases, antibiotics, organ transplants, splitting the atom, the automobile, the airplane, radio, television, the computer, space travel . . . these are just a few of the developments of man which evidence that we are living in those last days foretold by Daniel when knowledge and communications would increase. Michael informed Daniel that in these days when the time drew near for God to set up a kingdom on earth that would never pass away, the prophet's sealed book would be unsealed.

The primary purpose in writing this commentary on Daniel is to alert Christians, and non-believers alike, that the time of great tribulation spoken of by Jesus Christ is at hand. Our Lord Himself indicated that those living when that dreadful day approached should be reading the prophecies of Daniel in order to

i

discern the signs of His coming (Matt. 24:15).

But even as rapid a rate as knowledge has increased, as we approach the dawning of the seventh millennium, political changes are coming even faster. Daniel said again of the last days, *". . . the end thereof shall be with a flood. . . ."* Of the sudden breakup of communist puppet governments in East Europe, one national newscaster remarked, "It appears that God has pushed the fast-forward on history." President Bush remarked, as reported in the December 26, 1989 edition of *The Daily Oklahoman*, "We live in exciting times. The rapidity of change is mind-boggling."

The uniting of Europe once more into a Revived Roman Empire in 1992, as prophesied in the second chapter of Daniel, is just one of the many prophecies in Daniel that most likely will come to pass within the next decade. We are indeed fortunate to live in these exciting times, to be climaxed by the most exciting event of history: the coming of Jesus Christ in all His glory, as lightning shining from east to west, to take the problems of this world upon His shoulders.

This book is written about the life, times, and prophecies of Daniel, a man beloved of God. The style of writing is simplistic and conversational so that every reader, regardless of the educational level, will understand the message.

Chapter One

We begin our study on Daniel with the first two verses: *"In the third year of the reign of Jehoiakim king of Judah came Nebuchadnezzar king of Babylon unto Jerusalem, and besieged it. And the Lord gave Jehoiakim king of Judah into his hand, with part of the vessels of the house of God: which he carried into the land of Shinar to the house of his god; and he brought the vessels into the treasure house of his god"* (Dan. 1:1-2).

The conquest of Jerusalem by the king of Babylon signified God's complete and utter displeasure with the nation of Israel. According to the covenants that God made with Abraham and David, Israel would become the head of a mighty and everlasting theocratic kingdom on earth. The King over this kingdom would be called the Lord their God. Jerusalem would become the capital city of the world; the law would go forth from Jerusalem and there would be peace and prosperity in all nations. According to God's schedule for bringing in this kingdom, called the kingdom of Heaven, the seed of Abraham must first be prepared for the land. The preparation of the people for the land began in Egypt. It was in Egypt that the children of Israel, also called Jacob, fled to escape a great famine and to find food to sustain life. But even in a strange land the children of Israel remained racially pure. They did not believe in mixed marriages. This was a sign that God had separated them from the rest of the world for a particular purpose. This remains a peculiar property of the Jewish race even today. After wandering almost two thousand years in the nations of the world, the Jew remains a Jew. This fact continues to illustrate that God is not finished with Israel; they are still separated for that purpose which God determined when he covenanted with Abraham: *"I say then, Hath God cast away his people? God forbid. For I also am an Israelite, of the seed of Abraham, of the tribe of Benjamin"* (Rom. 11:1). An Israelite will always trace his beginning back to Abraham to indicate that he is an heir of the covenant. God is not finished with Israel. Had He been finished with them, He would have let the race die out within the Gentile nations of the world during this dispensation.

The race actually began with the twelve sons of Jacob, who was also called Israel. Jacob was a grandson of Abraham. In Egypt the children of Israel were very prolific. After several generations, they numbered in the hundreds of thousands; however, they were never considered citizens of Egypt. They were foreigners dwelling in alien territory; they were a people without a country. God had promised Abraham that He would bless his seed and they would multiply as the sand on the shore by the sea. After four hundred years there were so many Israelites in Egypt they became a real problem. They had taken over the richest land in that country, the Nile delta called the Land of Goshen. This area lies just west of the Suez Canal and inland about ninety miles. So the ruler of Egypt, called the pharaoh, issued an order that all the male babies be killed at birth. The government of Egypt made slaves of the Israelites and put them to work in public projects.

When they became downtrodden and abused, they remembered that there was a God with whom the head of the race, Abraham, had made an agreement. And so in their misery they cried out for deliverance. God heard their cries and sent them a leader, Moses, to lead them out of Egypt. Their deliverance came not by their own power and might, but by mighty miracles and signs. This was proof to the Israelites that God was with them and would make a mighty nation of them. *"Egypt was glad when they departed: for the fear of them fell upon them. He spread a cloud for a covering; and fire to give light in the night. The people asked, and he brought quails, and satisfied them with the bread of heaven. He opened the rock, and the waters gushed out; they ran in the dry places like a river. For he remembered his holy promise, and Abraham his servant"* (Ps. 105:38-42).

We read also from the sermon of Stephen to Israel in Acts 7:36: *"He brought them out, after that he had shewed wonders and signs in the land of Egypt, and in the Red sea and in the wilderness forty years."* All through the Old Testament, into the New Testament, and in synagogues today, Israelites still proclaim their miraculous deliverance from Egypt as a sign that God prepared them for a special land. After they were delivered from Egypt, God prepared a land for the people, the land of Palestine. But the people backslid and became fainthearted, and so God tested them in the wilderness for forty years. This wilderness in which they wandered most of the time was the Sinai Peninsula.

Finally, under the leadership of Joshua, the remnant of Israel crossed the Jordan to possess the land. But before the job was finished, they became tired of fighting. They wanted to settle down, build a house, raise a family, plant a garden, and sit in the shade of a mustard tree. So they compromised God's commandment and made friends with the remaining natives of the land. Though the people had been prepared for the land, and the land prepared for the people, the covenant with Abraham was delayed; they were delayed again under the administration of the judges; again under the administration of kings; set aside completely during the dispensation of grace; and yet even today Israel is not ready to accept its kingdom responsibility. As this dispensation began to draw to a close, God had to start all over. World War I prepared the land for the people; World War II prepared the people for the land; and this time, God will truly prepare the nation for the kingdom. The nation will be prepared for the King and the kingdom during the time of suffering and tribulation which they have not experienced to this date. It was prophesied by Jesus in Matthew 24:21: *"For then shall be great tribulation, such as was not since the beginning of the world to this time, no, nor ever shall be."*

We read in the book of Revelation that the Antichrist will turn on Israel to literally wipe every Jew off the face of the earth, but then God will spread wings over a remnant and miraculously protect them in a place called "the wilderness." This will be accomplished with miracles far greater than the miracles that God performed when He called them out of Egypt. So great will be the suffering of the Israelites during this time, and so miraculous will be their deliverance by God that they will all cry with one accord that they are ready to obey all of God's law; they will be ready to fulfill their part of the covenant that was made between God and the fathers of Israel; and they will be made ready to accept their King, the Lord Jesus Christ when He comes to place His feet upon the Mount of Olives and reign on David's throne. Jesus said to Israel: *". . . Ye shall not see me henceforth, till ye shall say, Blessed is he that cometh in the name of the Lord"* (Matt. 23:39).

The setting for the book of Daniel is cast in one of the darkest periods of Israel's history. A revolution that split the nation into two divisions had taken place in 975 B.C. at the end of the reign of Israel's third king, King Solomon. The cause for this rebellion is recorded in 2 Chronicles chapter ten. The main reasons were religious apostasy and excessive taxation. The nation was divided into two parts — Israel, the northern kingdom composed of ten tribes, and Judah, the southern kingdom made up of two tribes, Judah and Benjamin. The northern kingdom apostatized more than the southern kingdom, and for almost three hundred years there was civil strife as king after king sat upon the thrones of both Judah and Israel. Finally, God could look no longer upon the sins of Israel and He turned His face from them as the Assyrian Empire conquered and ravaged the land, even from Dan to Bethel. A remnant of the ten tribes of the northern kingdom escaped into Judah; thousands were taken into captivity to Nineveh, and aliens were imported by the Assyrians to mix with those remaining in the land. This was done by the enemy so that Israel might be destroyed as both a country and a people. However, as the Assyrians moved southward to capture Jerusalem, the capital city of Judah, the Lord intervened, the invading army was destroyed, and Judah was given a period of grace to repent and return to the keeping of the ordinance of the law. Less than one hundred years after the Assyrian invasion of Israel, the Babylonian Empire, which had absorbed the Assyrian Empire, came against Judah and captured Jerusalem.

Jehoiakim was king of Judah at the time that Nebuchadnezzar marched his army into the Holy City. Jehoiakim was a foolish man. He lacked moral courage and religious appreciation. He had no sympathy for the poor and reversed the reforms begun by his father, Josiah. He returned to the worship of idols and his most evil deed was the burning of a roll containing the sacred Word of God. His end is recorded as a warning to all nations and peoples who hold the sacred Scriptures in contempt. At first he attempted to make a deal with Nebuchadnezzar, then after he had delivered the city to him, he broke his agreement and attacked the Babylonians. He was put to death by Nebuchadnezzar and his body was left to decay on the ground outside the gates of Jerusalem.

The fall of Judah before Babylon was prophesied first by Isaiah and later by Jeremiah. The fall of Jerusalem recorded in Daniel 2:1-2 was the first time Jerusalem was taken by Nebuchadnezzar. Twice the city revolted, but each time it was captured and the city was dealt with more harshly. The temple of the Lord had been profaned with idols, and God allowed the Babylonians to completely destroy it. The destruction of the temple and the carrying of the holy vessels back to Babylon by Nebuchadnezzar indicated that the promises of the covenant had been set aside.

Josephus gives us an account of this event in his *History of the Jews*:

". . . The king of Babylon sent Nebuzaradan, the general of his army, to Jerusalem, to pillage the temple, who had it also in command to burn it and the royal palace, and to lay the city even with the ground, and to transplant the people into

Babylon. Accordingly, he came to Jerusalem and pillaged the temple, and carried out the vessels of God, both gold and silver, and particularly that large laver which Solomon dedicated, as also the pillars of brass, and their chapiters, with the golden tables and candlesticks; and when he had carried these off, he set fire to the temple in the eighteenth year of Nebuchadnezzar; he also burnt the palace, and overthrew the city. Now the temple was burnt four hundred and seventy years, six months, and ten days after it was built. It was then one thousand and sixty-two years, six months, and ten days from the departure out of Egypt. . . . The general of the Babylonian king now overthrew the city to the very foundations, and removed all the people, and took for prisoners the priest Seraiah, and Zephaniah the priest that was next to him, and the rulers that guarded the temple, who were three in number, and the eunuch who was over the armed men . . . and sixty other rulers; all which, together with the vessels they had pillaged, he carried to the king of Babylonia. . . . So the king commanded the heads of the high priest and of the rulers to be cut off there. . . ."

Thus, we can understand the plight of young Daniel as he finds himself in Babylon. Such is the setting for the book.

"And the king spake unto Ashpenaz the master

of his eunuchs, that he should bring certain of the children of Israel, and of the king's seed, and of the princes; Children in whom was no blemish, but well favoured, and skilful in all wisdom, and cunning in knowledge, and understanding science, and such as had ability in them to stand in the king's palace, and whom they might teach the learning and the tongue of the Chaldeans. And the king appointed them a daily provision of the king's meat, and of the wine which he drank: so nourishing them three years, that at the end thereof they might stand before the king. Now among these were of the children of Judah, Daniel, Hananiah, Mishael, and Azariah: Unto whom the prince of the eunuchs gave names: for he gave unto Daniel the name of Belteshazzar; and to Hananiah, of Shadrach; and to Mishael, of Meshach; and to Azariah, of Abednego" (Dan. 1:3-7).

The Babylon of Nebuchadnezzar was in reality a revival of the Babel of Nimrod. They were both built on the same site with the same ambitious program in mind. Nimrod started a space program whereby he could eventually traverse the heavens. God considered the project and realized that what man had determined in his heart to do, he could accomplish. And so God went down to Babel and confounded their speech and scattered them abroad over the face of the earth.

We have little difficulty in establishing the Tower of Babel as an historic reality, nor the fact that there was a ruler named Nimrod. It also appears evident that something happened to the language of this particular civilization. *Halley's Bible Handbook* states:

> *"It is commonly thought by archaeologists that more likely the actual site was the center of Babylon (where the Tower of Babel once stood), and identified with the ruins just north of the Marduk Temple. G. Smith found an ancient tablet reading: 'The building of this illustrious tower offended the gods. In a night they threw down what they had built. They scattered them abroad, and made strange their speech.'"*

The ancient Mound of Nimrod still stands near the site of Nineveh and Birs Nimrud, the Temple of Nimrod. Other historic sites which were named after Nimrod have been located.

When God stopped the building of the Tower of Babel, it is evident that He did more than divide the speech of the people into many languages. He also divided their intellect and talents according to the races. Even today there are degrees of intelligence and occupational aptitudes that are common to each race. Thus, after Babel, God made it difficult for the various races to get together again and pool their resources, intelligence, and talents to again launch an ambitious program of space travel. This does not mean that the Tower of Babel would have actually become a gateway to the heavens. We do not know whether the principles behind this program were scientifically sound or not; nor do we know exactly what plans were involved. However, man began dreaming about flying in the sky like the birds centuries ago. They made wings for themselves, and would flap them like birds do. They made huge kites; and every other conceivable plan imaginable. Finally, man succeeded. In our own space program, the scientists and engineers made several attempts before they were able to get a satellite into orbit. We would not contend with anyone that the Tower of Babel would have launched men into the heavens, but it was the plan behind the project that God considered to be vain, foolish, and contrary to His will: *"And the Lord said, Behold, the people is one, and they have all one language; and this they begin to do: and now nothing will be restrained from them, which they have imagined to do"* (Gen. 11:6). God knew that with man's entire capabilities dedicated to a program of inhabiting other planets in the heavens, he would ultimately succeed.

At the second Babel, which was called Babylon, the plan and program was revived. We read in Daniel chapter four about Nebuchadnezzar's dream concerning his own personal tree that grew up into Heaven, and then a watcher and a holy one, two officials in the universal government of God, came and cut the tree down. The dream indicated that Nebuchadnezzar planned to reinstitute the ambitious program of Nimrod. Daniel chapter one implies that the king brought to Babylon from the conquered nations the best educated, the most intelligent, and above all, those who had an understanding of science. These foreign intellectuals were separated for three years in a special school where they studied the language of the Chaldeans. They were all to speak a common language whereby they all might pool their knowledge and talents to fulfill the dream of Nebuchadnezzar. It was Babel all over again.

Our own nation is made up of people from every race, creed, and color, and we have a common language. All the intelligence and talents of the various races are combined in one nation. The world has never seen a nation like the United States — we are the leader in engineering, manufacturing, science, and technological skills. In addition, scientists have been brought in from many other nations to work in our space program. Again, we have the same situation that existed in Babel, and our leaders have dreamed the dream that Nebuchadnezzar dreamed. There is one exception. Where Nimrod and Nebuchadnezzar failed, we have succeeded — at least to a point. Although Russia has succeeded in launching satellites around the earth, and sent space vehicles to Venus and the moon, no Russian has set foot on a planet other than earth. Even though the United States has scored a space triumph in sending men to the moon, God could intervene at any time just as He did at Babel. We read in the book of Revelation of a third Babel, a great and mighty nation called Babylon in the extremity of the age. This third Babylon is described as being destroyed in a single day in what would appear to be a nuclear holocaust. Some think the Babylon that will be destroyed in a day is the United States. We do not like to think that it is, but it is possible. The analogy between the last Babylon and the United States is quite apparent.

In Daniel 1:6, we read that after the fall of Jerusalem, four budding young scientists were taken back captive to Babylon. Their names were Daniel, Hananiah, Mishael, and Azariah. They were not treated as ordinary captives. They were assigned the best living quarters and they were given the same food the king ate, the best in the land, and the same wine that he drank.

There was one exception to the royal care of these four young men — the king made eunuchs of them. This had been prophesied one hundred and six years prior to this time by the prophet Isaiah: *"Then came Isaiah the prophet unto king Hezekiah, and said unto him, What said these men? and from whence came they unto thee? And Hezekiah said, They are come from a far country, even from Babylon. And he said, What have they seen in thine house? And Hezekiah answered, All the things that are in mine house have they seen: there is nothing among my treasures that I have not shewed them. And Isaiah said unto Hezekiah, Hear the word of the Lord. Behold, the days come, that all that is in thine house, and that which thy fathers have laid up in store unto this day, shall be carried into Babylon: nothing shall be left, saith the Lord. And of thy sons that shall issue from thee, which thou shalt beget, shall they take away; and they shall be eunuchs in the palace of the king of Babylon. Then said Hezekiah unto Isaiah, Good is the word of the Lord which thou hast spoken. And he said, Is it not good, if peace and truth be in my days?"* (2 Kings 20:14-19).

The king and his cabinet invited godless foreigners in with open arms. They were invited into the palace; they were shown the military strength of the country. Hezekiah was a pretty good king — a hale-fellow-well-met who never met a foreigner he didn't trust. When he was entertaining this delegation from Babylon and revealing to them state secrets, Isaiah, the prophet of God came into the conference room. Isaiah warned the king that these foreigners were up to no good — they had plans to conquer the whole world, including Judah, and when they were strong enough to carry out these plans, they would conquer his country, destroy the cities, kill the people, and carry the young men back to Babylon as slaves and make eunuchs of them.

And so one hundred and six years later, we see the fruit of Judah, the most intelligent and best physical specimens of its young men, taken back to Babylon just as Isaiah prophesied, to be made eunuchs and become slaves of the state.

God's Word is sure. The pattern of human behavior has not changed. What costly mistakes and tragedies could be averted if we would heed the counsel that God gives us through the written Word, the Holy Bible.

When Babylon conquered Judah, the king commanded that all the young men who were considered excellent physical specimens, and who had a good education, especially in the field of science, should be brought back to the city of Babylon.

Daniel, one of the few men in the Bible against whom there is recorded no fault, was a Jew. The term "Jew" to designate the national identity of an Israelite from the kingdom of Judah, originated during the Babylonian captivity. They are repeatedly referred to as Jews in the books of Esther, Jeremiah, and Zechariah. We read in the Bible that after the Assyrian conquest of the northern kingdom, some members of the other ten tribes continued to come to the Passover in Jerusalem, and many of them doubtless settled in Judah to escape the Assyrians. Even though there were Israelites of every tribe in Judah, gradually all Israelites came to be called Jews.

During the three years that these four young Jews were attending school to learn the language of Babylon, they were also to be brainwashed. When they were to be brought before the king after three years, all the political and religious concepts which they inherited from their native country were to have been washed from their minds. In its place was to be implanted the religious and political ideology of Babylon.

Most Hebrew names held a religious significance, so it is understandable, if the Babylonians were to get these young men to turn from the faith of their fathers and accept the religion of Babylon, they would have to change their names. If they kept their original given names, they would have a constant reminder of the God of Abraham, Isaac, and Jacob. In Hebrew, *Daniel* signified "judged for God"; *Hananiah* meant "gift of the Lord"; *Mishael* meant "who is what God is"; and *Azariah* meant "whom Jehovah helps." Their overseer, the prince of the eunuchs, gave them Babylonian names. Daniel was renamed *Belteshazzar*, which meant "prince of Bel," the chief Babylonian deity. Hananiah was renamed *Shadrach*, which meant "the servant of Sin," the moon god. Mishael was renamed *Meshach*, which meant "who is what Aku is." Aku was the Sumerian equivalent of Sin. Azariah was renamed *Abednego*, which meant in the Chaldean language "servant of Nebo." Nebo was one of the gods that Nimrod worshipped, and perhaps the most prominent of the gods of Babel. Many Babylonian names carried the prefix Nebo, or Nebu. Nebuchadnezzar's name meant "the prince favored by Nebo." These names of religious significance carried over from ancient Babel offer substantiation to the belief that Babylon was actually a revival of the program which started at Babel for man to join Satan in his rebellion against the Most High God in the heavens.

These young men from Judah were separated and their training, whereby they were to forget all about their own heritage and traditions and become good Chaldeans, was begun. But we read in the Bible that if a child is trained in the way he should go in the home by his parents, that after he comes of age, he will not depart from it. And so we read in Daniel 1:8-9: *"But Daniel purposed in his heart that he would not defile himself with the portion of the king's meat, nor with the wine which he drank: therefore he requested of the prince of the eunuchs that he might not defile himself. Now God had brought Daniel into favour and tender love with the prince of the eunuchs."*

In Babylon and other nations of the Middle East, with the exception of Israel, it was according to their religions to sacrifice animals to idols. They would select the finest young cattle and fatten them up until they were prime beef or lamb. The fine animals were placed on an altar before the idol and a fire was started. After this choice beef and lamb had been roasted to perfection before the idol, it was removed to the king's kitchen and there the palace chef seasoned it, and these tantalizing platters of barbecue were served to the king and his company, along with all sorts of bread, fruit, vegetables, and the choicest wine.

This was the food that Daniel and the other young Jewish intellectuals were fed. This was their diet selected by the king. No one else in all the kingdom ate so well. But there was one thing wrong with this food. It had been offered up to idols and Daniel had been taught that God forbade Hebrews to eat anything that had been sacrificed to alien gods. This was spiritual abomination and the grossest apostasy in God's sight. This was one of the restrictions that James and Peter entreated Paul to place upon

Gentile Christians — to forbid them to eat meats polluted by idols (Acts 15:20).

Daniel informed his Babylonian caretaker, Ashpenaz, that he had no intention of eating any food from the king's table. We are told that he purposed this in his heart.

Daniel would have had a perfect excuse had he decided to eat the king's meat. After all, he was in a foreign land, he was separated from his family — they would not have known a thing about it. Also, there was the possibility that unless he did exactly what they wanted him to do, the guards would run a spear through him. The Babylonians didn't mess around with anybody — they were cruel and heartless. But the true test of moral strength in a person's character is that even if no one else in the whole world knows, and regardless of the cost, you are going to do what you know to be right.

We continue by reading Daniel 1:10-15: *"And the prince of the eunuchs said unto Daniel, I fear my lord the king, who hath appointed your meat and your drink: for why should he see your faces worse liking than the children which are of your sort? then shall ye make me endanger my head to the king. Then said Daniel to Melzar, whom the prince of the eunuchs had set over Daniel, Hananiah, Mishael, and Azariah, Prove thy servants, I beseech thee, ten days; and let them give us pulse to eat, and water to drink. Then let our countenances be looked upon before thee, and the countenances of the children that eat the portion of the king's meat: and as thou seest, deal with thy servants. So he consented to them in this matter, and proved them ten days. And at the end of ten days their countenances appeared fairer and fatter in flesh than all the children which did eat the portion of the king's meat."*

The king's officer put his own life in jeopardy by agreeing to Daniel's proposition, because should Nebuchadnezzar have come into their quarters and found four of his young Jewish intellectuals looking pale and haggard, he would have been killed. But Ashpenaz agreed only to a ten-day trial period. If at any time they began to lose weight or become pale of countenance, he would stop their diet of pulse and they would either eat the king's meat or starve.

This does not mean that Hebrews did not eat meat. They could eat fish, beef, lamb, goat, and several kinds of fowl. Daniel and his companions refused to eat any living thing in Babylon to rule out the possibility of ever eating anything that had been offered to idols. Pulse in the Hebrew means almost any type of edible vegetables, fruits, or nuts. So we see that the protein in their diet was compensated for by dates and nuts, and at the end of the trial period the four young Jews had actually gained weight and were healthier than any of their Hebrew companions.

"As for these four children, God gave them knowledge and skill in all learning and wisdom: and Daniel had understanding in all visions and dreams. Now at the end of the days that the king had said he

should bring them in, then the prince of the eunuchs brought them in before Nebuchadnezzar. And the king communed with them; and among them all was found none like Daniel, Hananiah, Mishael, and Azariah: therefore stood they before the king. And in all matters and wisdom and understanding, that the king inquired of them, he found them ten times better than all the magicians and astrologers that were in all his realm. And Daniel continued even unto the first year of king Cyrus" (Dan. 1:17-21).

Before we continue further in our study of the book of Daniel, we should become better acquainted with the author and the central figure of this prophecy — Daniel himself. We have already learned that Daniel was a devout servant of the Most High God, and he had strong moral convictions and strength of character. He was faithful to his beliefs. He did not say one thing and do another. He valued his own personal convictions more than he did physical life.

Here in Daniel 1:17 we are given some additional insight concerning the type of man Daniel was. We read that he was a man of knowledge and skill, a man who learned quickly and whose learning was varied. In other words, his interest and knowledge was not just confined to one field. He knew something about everything — sports, politics, theology, and various skills. And last but not least, we read that God gave him wisdom.

Now, what is wisdom? We read the definition given in *Webster's Dictionary: "The quality of being wise; the power of judging rightly and following the soundest course of action, based on knowledge, experience, and understanding."* Wisdom is often called "horse sense." Wisdom is the unique and rare ability which enables a person to take a set of facts, evaluate the information, and arrive at a logical conclusion. Regardless of how much education a person has or how much knowledge he has amassed, knowledge and all the degrees in the world will avail him little unless he has the wisdom to make use of that which he knows. It is not so much what you know, but rather how you use it. Misguided knowledge can be the most dangerous thing in the world. There are millions of young people in our colleges who will never be able to use constructively that which they are learning. Businessmen everywhere are looking for college graduates who can judge a situation and arrive at the soundest course of action.

At the end of the three-year schooling and training period, Daniel and his companions were brought before the king. Nebuchadnezzar communed with them, or as we would say today, he interviewed them to find out if they would be an asset to his government. Nebuchadnezzar was certainly no fool, and we read in verse twenty that he was not as much concerned about the grades they made as he was about their degree of wisdom and understanding. If an employee lacks knowledge in a certain field, he or she can always be taught or trained, but wisdom is something that is not learned from a textbook. At the

conclusion of the interview Nebuchadnezzar determined that Daniel, Hananiah, Mishael, and Azariah
were ten times better than anyone else in the entire
nation of Babylon on matters that required sound
judgment. As we would say today, these four young
Jews were top executive material.

But in addition to a keen and perceptive mind, we
read in verse seventeen that Daniel had something else
going for him. God had given him the ability to
understand visions and dreams. In the Bible we find
twenty-four people who dreamed dreams of sufficient
spiritual or prophetic importance to be recorded in
the Bible. These twenty-four people dreamed thirty-
four separate dreams (twenty-two in the Old
Testament; twelve in the New Testament). Some of
these people were godly people and others were
ungodly. It is apparent from Scripture that God did
reveal great prophetic truths to these people. Jacob
dreamed about a ladder that would reach up to
Heaven; Joseph was a dreamer and his brothers hated
him because God so favored him; the great prophecy
about the Gentile empires that would rise up in the
world was revealed to Nebuchadnezzar in a dream; an
angel appeared to Joseph in a dream to reveal that the
child Mary would bring into the world would be a
great and holy personality; Joseph was also warned in
a dream about the plan of Herod to kill all the babies;
and Pilate's wife was warned in a dream that her
husband should have nothing to do with the plot to
kill Jesus. These are just a few of the notable dreams

mentioned in the Bible. But just as God speaks to men in dreams, so does the devil. We read in Ecclesiastes 5:7: *"For in the multitude of dreams and many words there are also divers vanities. . . ."* We read in Jeremiah 23:27 that the prophets of Israel were misled in dreams to believe that their god was Baal. Zechariah 10:2 also speaks of diviners, spirit mediums, conjuring up false dreams. There is indeed a mystical relationship between dreams and the spirit world, and Daniel had the spiritual perception to determine whether a dream was of God or the devil and to decipher its meaning.

The Scriptures afford us some insight into why Daniel possessed this extremely sensitive spiritual gift. For three years he had not had one bit of meat, and there is a relationship between abstinence from meat and a sensitiveness to the spirit realm. Meat in its broadest sense means food of any kind — animal or vegetable. However, we use the word today in its modern meaning — animal flesh. We read in Genesis 1:29 that Adam ate no animal flesh. God had forbidden it. And Adam communed directly with God. We do not imply this was the only reason why the first man could talk directly with God, but it is a point to be considered. Also, from Adam to the flood, no man ate any flesh. Enoch walked with God, but there were millions of others who did not. We read in Genesis 6:2 of the invasion of angels that corrupted all flesh with the exception of Noah. Without doubt, the people before the flood were more susceptible to spiritual contacts than we are today, but to be spiritually sensitive does not mean a person will be open to the things of God. He could be deceived into having spiritual intercourse with the agents of Satan. This is what happened to the Antediluvians.

After the flood, God took corrective measures. He instituted human government whereby the death penalty was required for murder. This was to prevent the utter chaos that developed before the flood from happening again. He also commanded man to eat meat. We read in Genesis 9:3: *"Every moving thing that liveth shall be meat for you; even as the green herbs have I given you all things."* It would seem that this commandment would dull the spiritual senses of man where they might not become overly involved with the unseen spirit world. In Colossians 2:16 Paul admonishes Christians to let no one deter them in the eating of meat, and then in verse eighteen, he warns that we are not to be beguiled in the worship of angels. Paul also relates abstinence from meats to spiritual intercourse in 1 Timothy 4:1-3: *"Now the Spirit speaketh expressly, that in the latter times some shall depart from the faith, giving heed to seducing spirits, and doctrines of devils; Speaking lies in hypocrisy; having their conscience seared with a hot iron; Forbidding to marry, and commanding to abstain from meats. . . ."* Many of the spiritualist mediums do not eat meat.

Daniel, while in Babylon, ate no meat. Not by choice, but because he was fearful of eating meat that had been sacrificed to idols. It is little wonder that he could discern dreams and talk with angels. However, because of his deep faith and dedication to God, the Lord watched over him and protected him — not only from evil men, but from the princes of Satan.

Chapter Two

These four young Jews were paid the supreme compliment which the secular world could afford. And so the career of Daniel and his friends in the court of the king of Babylon began. But they soon found that life in the king's palace was no bed of roses, and it could be exceedingly dangerous at times. *"And in the second year of the reign of Nebuchadnezzar Nebuchadnezzar dreamed dreams, wherewith his spirit was troubled, and his sleep brake from him. Then the king commanded to call the magicians, and the astrologers, and the sorcerers, and the Chaldeans, for to shew the king his dreams. So they came and stood before the king. And the king said unto them, I have dreamed a dream, and my spirit was troubled to know the dream. Then spake the Chaldeans to the king in Syriak, O king, live for ever: tell thy servants the dream, and we will shew the interpretation. The king answered and said to the Chaldeans, The thing is gone from me: if ye will not make known unto me the dream, with the interpretation thereof, ye shall be cut in pieces, and your houses shall be made a dunghill"* (Dan. 2:1-5).

There is much disagreement among noted scholars like Rev. Larkin, Dr. Newell, Dr. Talbot, Dr. DeHaan, and many others as to just when the king dreamed this dream. Some believe it was the same year that Daniel was taken to Babylon, another the second year, and yet another the fifth year, and so on. It actually makes very little difference at what date, in relation to Daniel's stay in Babylon, the king dreamed this dream. The Scriptures do not say the king wanted it interpreted the day after he dreamed it. Inasmuch as he dreamed it in the second year of his reign, it seems apparent that he must have waited two or three years before he began to worry about it. This would explain why he had forgotten it.

Astrology was one of the four classes of the occult which Nebuchadnezzar relied on for guidance in helping him to make decisions. Astrologers were also called stargazers and they were very much like the astrologers today. They would come in to the king and tell him whether he would be positive that day and win friends and influence people, or should go back to bed and pull the covers over his head. In other words, they provided his daily horoscope. Next came the sorcerers. In ancient manuscripts they are called the "mutterers of magic formulae." They used drugs and potions to deceive the mind. The root word for sorcery is the same word from which pharmacy or drugs is derived. It would appear that the magicians or wizards of those days corresponded to the male counterpart of a witch. They performed all kinds of miracles including consultations with the dead. The Chaldeans were from the province of Chaldea, located in the southern part of Babylonia along the Euphrates river. As best as Bible scholars can determine, they were the remnant of the Tower of Babel society who did not experience a change in language. They composed a priesthood that continued to commune with the gods of Babel.

When these so-called wise men were assembled, the king came in and addressed them in the Syriac, the ancient Syrian language. That part which refers directly to Israel was written in Hebrew, and that part which relates to Babylon and the Gentile world empires was written in the old Syrian language, also called Aramaic. Critics of the Bible contend that Daniel did not write the book because a Hebrew would not have written in a foreign language. However, Daniel had just completed three years of study learning this language.

Even in his best mood, Nebuchadnezzar was not to be crossed, but on that morning he was completely out of sorts. He had experienced many sleepless nights, and probably that previous night he had not slept at all. He was going to resolve this matter so he could get some rest or heads were going to roll. The king is still speaking as we pick up the scripture in Daniel 2:6: *"But if ye shew the dream, and the interpretation thereof, ye shall receive of me gifts and rewards and great honour; therefore shew me the dream, and the interpretation thereof. They answered again and said, Let the king tell his servants the dream, and we will shew you the interpretation of it. The king answered and said, I know of certainty that ye would gain the time, because ye see the thing is gone from me. But if ye will not make known unto me the dream, there is but one decree for you: for ye have prepared lying and corrupt words to speak before me, till the time be changed: therefore tell me the dream, and I shall know that ye can shew me the interpretation thereof. The Chaldeans answered before the king, and said, There is not a man upon the earth that can shew the king's matter: therefore there is no king, lord, nor ruler, that asked such things at any magician, or astrologer, or Chaldean. And it is a rare thing that the king requireth, and there is none other that can shew it before the king, except the gods, whose dwelling is not with flesh. For this cause the king was angry and very furious, and commanded to destroy all the wise men of Babylon. And the decree went forth that the wise men should be slain; and they sought Daniel and his fellows to be slain"* (Dan. 2:6-13).

The exchange that occurred between the king and the wise men is self-explanatory. They could see that Nebuchadnezzar was in a bad way, and it is evident that the wise men had dealt with him in these angry moods before. They tried to gain a little time so he could cool off and perhaps think better of his rash decision on the morrow. But this time, the king was not to be placated. The Chaldeans came forth with a last minute plea. They protested that there was not a man on earth who could do what the king wanted, and they pointed out how unreasonable the king's request was. But the more they tried to reason with Nebuchadnezzar the more angry and furious he became until he ended the meeting by commanding his guards to round up every wise man in the kingdom for immediate execution.

No king had ever required of his subjects such an impossible task, but then again, there had never been a king like Nebuchadnezzar. He was the sole monarch over all nations that encompassed the civilized world. He had within his power the right to determine life or death. And how did he come into possession of such power? God gave it to him. We read in Jeremiah 27:4-8: "... *Thus saith the Lord of hosts, the God of Israel; Thus shall ye say unto your masters; I have made the earth, the man and the beast that are upon the ground, by my great power and by my outstretched arm, and have given it unto whom it seemed meet unto me. And now have I given all these lands into the hand of Nebuchadnezzar the king of Babylon, my servant; and the beasts of the field have I given him also to serve him. And all nations shall serve him, and his son, and his son's son, until the very time of his land come: and then many nations and great kings shall serve themselves of him. And it shall come to pass, that nation and kingdom which will not serve the same Nebuchadnezzar the king of Babylon, and that will not put their neck under the yoke of the king of Babylon, that nation will I punish, saith the Lord, with the sword, and with the famine, and with the pestilence, until I have consumed them by his hand.*"

Nebuchadnezzar was chosen of God for a particular work — to become the head of Gentile empires, and the entire duration of this would be known as the "times of the Gentiles." The king was chosen by God, the dream was given by God, and it was taken away by God. This was why these ungodly wise men, in spite of all their worldly wisdom, could not tell the king what he wanted to know. The reason is given in 1 Corinthians 2:14: *"But the natural man receiveth not the things of the Spirit of God; for they are foolishness unto him: neither can he know them, because they are spiritually discerned."*

We read next Daniel 2:14-18: *"Then Daniel answered with counsel and wisdom to Arioch the captain of the king's guard, which was gone forth to slay the wise men of Babylon: He answered and said to Arioch the king's captain, Why is the decree so hasty from the king? Then Arioch made the thing known to Daniel. Then Daniel went in, and desired of the king that he would give him time, and he would shew the king the interpretation. Then Daniel went to his house, and made the thing known to Hananiah, Mishael, and Azariah, his companions: That they would desire mercies of the God of heaven concerning this secret; that Daniel and his fellows should not perish with the rest of the wise men of Babylon."*

It would appear that the decree was given to Arioch, the captain of the king's guard, and an order went forth from him to the members of the guard to go throughout the city and round up every person that was covered within the context of the decree. We can imagine Daniel's surprise as he was suddenly arrested and informed of the charges against him and the penalty. A short time before, the king had praised him for his great wisdom. But now we see the wisdom of Daniel being proven and put to the test. He appraised the situation, considered the facts, and immediately arrived at a logical course of action. He did not have time to sit around and mull the matter over or think about it for several days. The decree was final and it was sudden. He had to act fast and he would be given only one chance to save his life and the lives of the other three men. Like it is today, when a man is arrested for a serious crime, Daniel was allowed one phone call.

Daniel knew it would only be adding fuel to the fire to ask the king to try to remember his dream, and he didn't try to reason with him or argue with him. Daniel knew the monarch would allow him only a few seconds, so he chose his words carefully and wisely. He spoke to the king and told him that if he would give him a little time, he would reveal the interpretation of the dream. The poise and self-assurance displayed by this young Jew gained the king's confidence, and gave God's servant the time requested. It would appear that he was given twenty-four hours to come up with the interpretation.

From Daniel 2:17 we know that all four of these young Jews lived in the same house, and so Daniel immediately departed to apprise his companions of the situation. Humanly speaking, Daniel agreed with the spokesman of the Chaldeans. There was no way he or any person could know the secret of the dream. It was simply an impossibility. But Daniel did know someone who would know the dream. He was the same person who had put the dream in Nebuchadnezzar's head, and He was God. If God would make known the dream of Daniel, he and his companions would live; otherwise, they would die.

We read in Daniel that the four young Jews got down on their knees before God for a session of prayer. They sought God's mercy in their behalf, because they knew if the dream was ever made known to them, it would be through the mercy and grace of the Lord. Here is an example of literally placing one's life in God's hands. *"Then was the secret revealed unto Daniel in a night vision. Then Daniel blessed the God of heaven"* (Dan. 2:19).

It is apparent that after they committed the matter to God in prayer, the burden was lifted from their minds and they went to bed. Sometime during the night God revealed to Daniel in the vision the very same thing that Nebuchadnezzar had seen in his dream. Daniel now had the information that would save their lives, but the Scriptures instruct us that in all things we are first to thank God. Before we eat we should thank God for the food which He has set before us. Therefore, Daniel knew before he went to the king with this knowledge he should first give thanks. *"Daniel answered and said, Blessed be the name of God for ever and ever: for wisdom and might are his: And he changeth the times and seasons: he removeth kings, and setteth up kings: he giveth wisdom unto the wise, and knowledge to them that know understanding: He revealeth the deep and secret things: he knoweth what is in the darkness, and the light dwelleth with him. I thank thee, and praise thee, O thou God of my fathers, who hast given me wisdom and might, and hast made known unto me now what we desired of thee: for thou hast now made known unto us the king's matter."*

Daniel acknowledged God as the ultimate and complete authority in seven things, and seven is the number of perfection.

1. God is the source of all wisdom and power.
2. God changes time and seasons — He can end one dispensation and bring in another; He changes the earth from the Garden of Eden to a place of war, drought, and famine, and then changes it back to Eden again.
3. He removes kings and heads of state and establishes new governments in order that His ultimate plan and purpose may be accomplished upon the earth.
4. To those who understand that there is a Divine Creator and that this Almighty God has a will for the universe, God will impart knowledge according to their ability to use knowledge.
5. God reveals the deep and secret things from the beginning of creation to the age of eternity for those who are humble and of a contrite spirit.

6. He gives wisdom to the wise. He entrusts responsibility and authority to those who are able to judge themselves as well as those who have the ability to profitably use that which God has given to their trust.

7. In God the source of all light dwells, and without Him darkness would fill the universe and all things therein would become without form and void — the stars and planets would be tumbling over each other in a state of utter chaos.

This is the God whom Daniel acknowledged and it is the God of Daniel whom we also address in our prayers. He is the God who is all-sufficient. Therefore, let us not limit His power. When we go to Him in prayer, let us be careful for nothing. There is no burden too heavy for Him to lift and no problem too perplexing for Him to solve.

"Therefore Daniel went in unto Arioch, whom the king had ordained to destroy the wise men of Babylon: he went and said thus unto him; Destroy not the wise men of Babylon: bring me in before the king, and I will shew the king the interpretation. Then Arioch brought in Daniel before the king in haste, and said thus unto him, I have found a man of the captives of Judah, that will make known unto the king the interpretation" (Dan. 2:24-25).

Although Daniel and his three countrymen had been given a brief reprieve, the execution of the sorcerers, astrologers, and Chaldeans was proceeding as ordered. A king, and especially a king as powerful as Nebuchadnezzar, could not void a decree without proper cause.

As Daniel entered the courtyard he rushed up to the captain of the guard and shouted as he came to halt the execution. He quickly informed Arioch that he had the dream and the interpretation, and the king's hatchetmen rushed him into the throneroom.

When Daniel and the captain of the king's guard appeared before the king, Arioch acted out the part of a typical bureaucrat by proudly announcing that he had found the answer to the king's problem. He declared that he had found the answer to the perplexing problem that harassed Nebuchadnezzar — he had after much searching and seeking located a man from among the Jewish captives who could reveal the king's dream. In any event, we know that Arioch didn't really have anything to do with finding Daniel, because it was Daniel who found him. The only part he had was in acting as a page to announce Daniel and make known his request for a royal audience with Nebuchadnezzar. *"The king answered and said to Daniel, whose name was Belteshazzar, Art thou able to make known unto me the dream which I have seen, and the interpretation thereof? Daniel answered in the presence of the king, and said, The secret which the king hath demanded cannot the wise men, the astrologers, the magicians, the soothsayers, shew unto the king; But there is a God in heaven that revealeth secrets, and maketh known to the king Nebuchadnezzar what shall be in the latter days. Thy dream, and the visions of thy head upon thy bed, are these; As for thee, O king, thy thoughts came into thy mind upon thy bed, what should come to pass hereafter: and he that revealeth secrets maketh known to thee what shall come to pass. But as for me, this secret is not revealed to me for any wisdom that I have more than any living, but for their sakes shall make known the interpretation to the king, and that thou mightest know the thoughts of thy heart"* (Dan. 2:26-30).

Once again Daniel displayed the wisdom which God had so abundantly endowed him with. He appraised the situation and arrived at the proper course of action. The essence of Daniel's opening remarks was that the king's dream concerned a great prophecy, a prophecy that extended from his day to the very last days. Daniel continued and explained that this dream had been given to the king by God in Heaven, and this was why the astrologers, the magicians, and the Chaldeans could not reveal it. They did not know this God of whom he spoke.

Throughout this presentation to the king, Daniel continued to divert Nebuchadnezzar's attention from himself to God. He took credit for nothing. He explained that he would not have known the dream except God revealed it to him. He gave all the honor and glory to the Lord, and herein lies the secret of how Daniel survived for seventy years in the royal court of Babylon. He always gave God the glory.

Daniel is an outstanding example of those who are greatly blessed of God, and He will bless and use those who honor Him instead of reaping glory for themselves. When Daniel gave God the glory, a heathen king even wanted to know this God who was so powerful that He could reveal a dream that he had already forgotten.

The importance of this dream to the history of the world is revealed in verse thirty. Daniel said that it was not for his sake or the king's sake only that God made known the dream, but for the sake of all living — meaning all who would live during the prophetic scope of its complete fulfillment. In other words, even for the sake of all men and women living today did God reveal this dream to Daniel. He did it so that you and I might have a fuller understanding of what is coming to pass upon the earth and the plan and purpose which God has for the world. The dream of Nebuchadnezzar, the head of the first great Gentile empire, is given in Daniel 2:31-35: *"Thou, O king, sawest, and behold a great image. This great image, whose brightness was excellent, stood before thee; and the form thereof was terrible. This image's head was of fine gold, his breast and his arms of silver, his belly and his thighs of brass, His legs of iron, his feet part of iron and part of clay. Thou sawest till that a stone was cut out without hands, which smote the image upon his feet that were of iron and clay, and brake them to pieces. Then was the iron, the clay, the brass, the silver, and the gold, broken to pieces together, and became like the chaff of the summer threshingfloors; and the wind carried them away, that no place was found for them: and the stone that smote the image became a great mountain, and filled the whole earth."*

As the king remained silent Daniel began to describe to him what he had seen in his dream, a metallic colossus. This giant image of a man was made of various types of metal which gradually decreased in value from its head downward to its feet, and at the end of the dream Nebuchadnezzar had seen a rock falling down from the sky and hit the image on its feet of iron and clay. Then the entire image began to break up in small pieces and then the pieces broke up and subdivided until there was nothing left but a pile of dust, and then the wind began to blow and the dust was carried away through the air until there was not a speck left. And as Nebuchadnezzar watched, the stone began to expand and increase in size until it covered the entire earth from pole to pole.

Daniel knew that this was the dream which the king had dreamed because as he continued the monarch doubtless began to recall what he had dreamed, and if it had not been right, the king would have stopped him and ordered him to be taken out and killed. At the conclusion Daniel said: *"This is the dream"* (Dan. 2:36). There was absolutely no doubt in his mind but that this was the correct description. And we begin to understand why Nebuchadnezzar was so troubled.

We are told that the meaning of Nebuchadnezzar's dream would have prophetic significance from the generation of Daniel's day to the very end of the age; therefore, it would hold a lesson for us today. If you were to ask most of the seminary graduates or modernistic preachers what lesson the image of Nebuchadnezzar's dream would have for us today, they would probably reply: "Don't build statues with clay feet, and watch out for those falling rocks." This is all the prophetic Word means to the vast majority of the clerics today, because they are carnally minded and cannot spiritually discern the revelations of God that came as the Holy Spirit moved upon the prophets to record what would come upon the earth in the ages to come.

Let us now continue and read the interpretation of the dream as given in Daniel 2:37-45: *"Thou, O king, art a king of kings: for the God of heaven hath given thee a kingdom, power, and strength, and glory. And wheresoever the children of men dwell, the beasts of the field and the fowls of the heaven hath he given into thine hand, and hath made thee ruler over them all. Thou art this head of gold. And after thee shall arise another kingdom inferior to thee, and another third kingdom of brass, which shall bear rule over all the earth. And the fourth kingdom shall be strong as iron: forasmuch as iron breaketh in pieces, and subdueth all things: and as iron that breaketh all these, shall it break in pieces and bruise. And whereas thou sawest the feet and toes, part of potters' clay, and part of iron, the kingdom shall be divided; but there shall be in it of the strength of the iron, forasmuch as thou sawest the iron mixed with miry clay. And as the toes of the feet were part of iron and part of clay, so the kingdom shall be partly strong, and partly broken. And whereas thou sawest iron mixed with miry clay, they shall mingle themselves with the seed of men: but they shall not cleave one to another, even as iron is not mixed with clay. And in the days of these kings shall the God of heaven set up a kingdom, which shall never be destroyed: and the kingdom shall not be left to other people, but it shall break in pieces and consume all these kingdoms, and it shall stand for ever. Forasmuch as thou sawest that the stone was cut out of the mountain without hands, and that it brake in pieces the iron, the brass, the clay, the silver, and the gold; the great God hath made known to the king what shall come to pass hereafter: and the dream is certain, and the interpretation thereof sure."*

Notice first that Nebuchadnezzar dreamed this dream because God put it in his head. Daniel said that God gave him the dream so that he, as well as you and I, might know what was coming upon the earth.

This dream did not relate to social, economic, ecological, or religious conditions. It related to only one phase of man's existence — human government. The Word of God is plain — the various metallic components of the image from the head to the toes referred to succeeding kingdoms, or empires.

The scope of this prophecy, according to time, was from the day that Nebuchadnezzar ascended to the throne of Babylon in 606 B.C. to the day that God would establish His kingdom on the earth. We still pray today: "Thy kingdom come, Thy will be done, on earth as it is in Heaven." The kingdom of Heaven has not been brought in upon earth in spite of what some teach, and according to Nebuchadnezzar's dream, it cannot be brought in until the last world empire is destroyed by the appearance of the great rock, and we shall establish without a doubt that the rock represents the Lord Jesus Christ.

As we survey the composition of this metallic monster, we find that it diminished in value from gold to clay. The head of gold, as we read in Scripture, was Nebuchadnezzar and the Babylonian Empire. But after Babylon, an inferior empire would arise, and then another and another until the last empire of man would be as iron mixed with clay. The gravity of gold is 19.5; of silver, 10.47; of brass, 8; of cast-iron, 5; of clay, 1.93. We are told that man is climbing up the evolutionary ladder, but the Word of God does not verify this theory.

The clay and iron mixed in the lower extremity of the image doubtless refers to the governmental composition of nations during the last days. The iron represents unbending dictatorships and the clay represents yielding democracies. You can take clay and change its shape almost at will, and this is the way democracies are. The people can change their governments almost at will, but like children playing with clay, they often get tired of the game and demand a king. It is true that a democracy can be the best type of government, but in all the history of mankind, it has never worked out this way. A democracy has always ended up being the worst possible type of government. A democracy that becomes corrupted with graft, greed, and public apathy is worse than no government at all. Israel had a democratic form of government until its judicial system became corrupted by judges who took bribes, and the people cried: "Give us a king."

Daniel tells us that the government of Babylon headed by Nebuchadnezzar was represented by the head of gold on the image. Gold is the most precious, costly, and concentrated of all metals. And humanly speaking, the government of Babylon was the most absolute of all governments that have been instituted upon the earth since that time. The government over which Nebuchadnezzar ruled was complete totalitarianism. He was given complete authority over every person in the known world at that time. Even the fish of the rivers and lakes, the birds that flew in the air, and the oxen, sheep, and even the wild deer and others animals belonged to him. If he had decreed that no one could catch a fish, that decree would have been carried out. His word was law and without recourse throughout the civilized world. Any person who broke or violated a decree of the king was executed. Any person or persons who failed to obey a commandment of the king, regardless of how absurd or impossible the commandment was, was put to death in a manner chosen by Nebuchadnezzar. All matter of government relating to law, religion, the social order, economics, and politics was administered from one government head. This was total government.

In 536 B.C. (or 538 B.C., depending upon the historical source), Babylon fell to the combined forces of two countries, Media and Persia. This new empire absorbed all the territories controlled by Babylon, and it became known as the Medo-Persian Empire. Nebuchadnezzar died in 561 B.C., and the empire disintegrated rapidly under the succession of royal heirs who were neither morally nor politically strong enough to keep the empire together. Thus, we see the second empire represented by the silver breast and arms on Nebuchadnezzar's image come into view. Media was represented by one arm, and Persia by the other arm. Because Media was the older of the two kingdoms, Cyrus, king of Persia, allowed his uncle, Darius, to have the position of leadership. But within two years, Cyrus became the sole monarch of both kingdoms as prophesied in Isaiah 44 and 45: *"That saith of Cyrus, He is my shepherd, and shall perform all my pleasure: even saying to Jerusalem, Thou shalt be built; and to the temple, Thy foundation shall be laid. Thus saith the Lord to his anointed, to Cyrus, whose right hand I have holden, to subdue nations before him; and I will loose the loins of kings* [as those of Belshazzar], *to open before him* [Cyrus] *the two leaved gates* [of Babylon]; *and the gates shall not be shut* [which was true of the inner gates of Babylon]

. . . For Jacob my servant's sake, and Israel mine elect, I have even called thee by thy name: I have surnamed thee, though thou hast not known me" (Isa. 44:28; 45:1, 4).

For Israel's sake, God brought an end to the Babylonian Empire after seventy years, because Jeremiah had prophesied that Judah would be in captivity for seventy years. Because silver is lesser in value and weight than gold, the Medo-Persian Empire was not as totalitarian in governmental structure as the Babylonian Empire.

Whereas Nebuchadnezzar had been the sole monarch with complete authority over all the kingdom, Cyrus was accountable to the nobles of the royal family who held lesser positions of honor in the provinces. The gold empire had been replaced by the silver empire.

We read of the brass king in Daniel 2:39: *"And after thee shall arise another kingdom inferior to thee, and another third kingdom of brass, which shall bear rule over all the earth."* It is said of Alexander that after he had conquered all the known world, he sat down and cried because there were no more worlds for him to conquer. Of course, we know that God did not speak through the prophets of Israel from 400 B.C. until the time of Christ; however, history records for us an amazing event relating to the part of Daniel's prophecy concerning the brass empire, which would be the same as the Grecian Empire. The Jewish historian Josephus relates that the king of the Persian

Empire did not consider Alexander to be a serious threat. Alexander had crossed over into Asia and defeated a Persian army which had been sent to keep him from crossing the Hellespont. Alexander, a gifted Grecian military leader employed a new concept of warfare with which the massive Persian army could not cope. So even when the main Persian army met him in combat it was defeated.

Judah at that time was still a province of the Medo-Persian Empire, and Alexander sent a courier to the chief high priest at Jerusalem informing him of the defeat of the Persian army. It was demanded of the chief high priest that he open the cities of Judah to the forces of Greece and be ready to cooperate with Alexander in every way possible. If this were done, then Alexander would deal kindly with the Jews and not disturb their provincial government or their religion. However, the chief high priest replied that the Jews were an honorable people and they had a covenant with the king of Persia, and as long as the king lived, they would observe the terms of the covenant. The army of Alexander was delayed seven months with the siege of Tyre and two months with mop-up operations at Gaza. But Alexander swore that as soon as it was militarily possible, he would go to Jerusalem and take vengeance upon the whole Jewish nation. Now the Syrians, who have always hated the Jews, and who have a long history of cowardly and traitorous conduct, were following behind the army of Alexander as it advanced upon

Jerusalem. They were eagerly awaiting the opportunity to pillage the city and kill the priests. From the account by Josephus, we determine:

1. The Chaldeans continued to be the enemies of the Jews. These were the descendants of the Chaldeans who plotted against Daniel in Nebuchadnezzar's court.

2. Alexander could have easily destroyed Jerusalem and killed all the Jews, but as God had done before, He interceded in behalf of the Jews by appearing to a heathen king in a dream.

3. Alexander himself acknowledged that his great military victories were according to a Divine plan, and unless God had willed it, he could not have defeated the greatly superior Persian army.

4. Alexander read the book of Daniel and understood that his kingdom was the brass empire on the image in Nebuchadnezzar's dream.

5. Alexander worshipped the God of Israel; he acknowledged his lost condition, and he offered up a sacrifice to God for his sins in the temple.

After the death of Alexander, the empire was divided into four divisions with each of the four top military generals given a province. Each province soon was ruled by different types of government, and in the extremity of the Grecian age, Greece itself became subject to the various political, moral, religious, social, and economic teachings of its great philosophers like Aristotle, Plato, and others. In its overall historical perspective, Greece was indeed a brass empire.

We come now to the fourth kingdom spoken of in the image of Nebuchadnezzar, the iron kingdom. *"And the fourth kingdom shall be strong as iron: forasmuch as iron breaketh in pieces and subdueth all things: and as iron that breaketh all these, shall it break in pieces and bruise"* (Dan. 2:40).

The Grecian Empire outlasted in time the Babylonian Empire and the Persian Empire mainly for the reason that no strong and ambitious alliance came into being to challenge the military might of Greece. The Semitic nations had been overthrown and weakened by Babylon, and then Greece overran the Hammitic nations. Greece was actually the first Japhetic empire to come into being. But after the Grecian Empire had existed in one form or another for three hundred years, it too began to decline. The Greeks grew tired of looking after the affairs of the world and upholding the responsibility that a world empire entails. But farther to the west another empire was growing and Greece showed no inclination to challenge it. This empire was Rome, and in 30 B.C. the legions of Rome marched through Egypt on their way to Israel and the Middle East. At the end of the year 30 B.C. all the known world lay either under, or within the power of Rome. Rome came into the Middle East to fill the vacuum left by a decaying Grecian Empire.

Within a year after Rome crossed over the Mediterranean Sea and began their march eastward, she had Israel and the entire Mediterranean area under her control. Time will not allow us to give a resume' of Roman history, but we know that the Roman Empire was divided into two parts, and the two legs on the image represent this division. All important prophetic locations are to the north of Israel, and by facing the image to the north, the left leg would represent the western division of Rome and the right leg would be the eastern division, encompassing almost all of the Middle East.

Let us notice very carefully what Daniel said will happen to the legs of iron: *"And the fourth kingdom shall be strong as iron; forasmuch as iron breaketh in pieces and subdueth all things; and as iron that breaketh all these, shall it break in pieces and bruise"* (Dan. 2:40).

In the chronological order of empires, the iron kingdom, or Rome, was to break up into pieces, and each iron piece would represent a nation. In other words, the Roman Empire has never ceased to exist. It has simply broken up into various independent nations.

The preservation of the Roman dictatorial form of government is evident in the two strongest nations in the eastern leg and the western leg today — Germany and Russia. Germany named its king *kaiser*, which is German for "caesar." Russia named its king *czar,* which is Russian for "caesar." The Bolshevik Revolution, which was taken over by the communists, replaced the government of Russian czars with a system of commissars, or communists "caesars."

Rome began to break up in A.D. 476 but endured in some form until A.D. 963 when its dissolution became a historical fact. Even so, as the prophecy of Daniel foretold, Rome continued to rule the world in its broken state. Each chunk of the iron in the legs became an empire: the Spanish Empire, the British Empire, the Dutch Empire, the Italian Empire, the Belgian Empire, the French Empire, etc.

Also, according to the prophecy of Daniel, the iron chunks from the broken legs would jostle against each other and bruise. History has recorded the literal fulfillment of this part of the prophecy: French-English wars; Spanish-English wars; the Napoleonic wars; and both World War I and World War II were started by European powers that were once integral parts of the old Roman Empire.

Many attempts have been made since A.D. 963 to put the humpty-dumpty Roman Empire back together again. Napoleon tried time and time again, yet he was never able to conquer England. Hitler tried, but he made the same mistake that Napoleon made — he tried to conquer Russia before taking England. According to the prophecy of Daniel, and related prophecies in Revelation, Rome would not be revived through conquest, but rather by common agreement. This prophecy has been fulfilled in our day through the Common Market Alliance.

It should be noted that according to the prophecy based on Nebuchadnezzar's dream, the iron pieces of Rome would eventually break up. This final disintegration of ancient Rome is represented by the pieces of iron and clay in the feet of the image, indicating that it would occur in the very extremity of the age. This occurred after World War II, and it came about mostly through agreements made by Joseph Stalin of Russia and Franklin Roosevelt. These two world leaders represented the two most powerful nations in the world to emerge from the second world holocaust. Winston Churchill of England protested to President Roosevelt that he could not agree with the extermination of the British Empire, but his protests availed little.

Almost immediately after World War II, the Roman colonial system began to break up. Colony after colony of France, England, Germany, Italy, Holland, Belgium, etc., gained or were granted independence. The only shadows of Rome that were left were a few nations with British commonwealth status like Canada, Australia, and New Zealand.

In our study of Daniel's interpretation of Nebuchadnezzar's dream, we have now come to the lowest extremity of the image — the toes. In considering the last part of the image, let us read again Daniel 2:42-43: *"And as the toes of the feet were part of iron, and part of clay, so the kingdom shall be partly strong, and partly broken. And whereas thou sawest iron mixed with miry clay, they shall mingle themselves with the seed of men: but they shall not cleave one to another, even as iron is not mixed with clay."*

First, we notice that these ten toes represent a kingdom in the very extremity of the age. We know that they will comprise a kingdom because we are told *"the kingdom shall be partly strong, and partly broken."* But what kingdom is Daniel speaking of here? He mentions the first kingdom, Babylon; the second kingdom, Medo-Persia; the third kingdom, Greece; the fourth kingdom, Rome. But when he gets to the toes, he does not say the fifth kingdom, but simply the kingdom. The reason Daniel did not identify the toes as a fifth kingdom is because he was still referring back to the fourth kingdom, Rome. In other words, verses forty through forty-three are all about the fourth kingdom. Even though the kingdom would break up into pieces and never cleave together again, the pieces themselves are still referred to as a kingdom. Even in the toes we find the iron and the clay mixed together. We refer to this ten-nation kingdom in the end of the age as the Revived Roman Empire.

Even after the final breakup of Rome there remained a need for an exchange of manufactured goods and agricultural products. Therefore, except in times of wars or political upheavals, a European fair was held yearly at Versailles, France. At these fairs produce of all kinds was brought by farmers and merchants to be exchanged or sold. Also, trade agreements were made. These fairs were called the "common market."

After World War II with the loss of colonies, the nations of Europe could no longer depend upon needed imports from these former territories. Therefore, the need for a revival of the "common market" concept arose. This need was consummated through a treaty in Rome binding Italy, France, Germany, Holland, Belgium, and Luxembourg to a "common market" agreement. By 1988, the alliance had grown to twelve nations with a common parliament and a president. Today, the Common Market alliance has a common passport, a common currency exchange, a common wage scale, a common military force through NATO, and though remaining independent nations, they act politically as a unit in dealing with the United States and Russia. The target date for the completion of a United States of Europe, which prophetically speaking would be the same as the Revived Roman Empire, is 1992.

Nebuchadnezzar had a dream. He dreamed that his Babylonian Empire would cover the entire earth and last forever. The king of Persia had a dream. Cyrus wanted to establish a kingdom that would control the world and last forever. Alexander the Great had a dream — and he actually thought he had conquered the world and that Greece would control all nations. Rome, likewise, envisioned an eternal empire, and its capital was called the eternal city and all roads led to Rome. Napoleon had a dream. The American Republic, the United States, had a dream. We were going to make the world safe for democracy. England had a dream, and for more than a century, the sun never set on the British Empire. Hitler had a dream — but where is Hitler and his dream today? Communism has a dream, but the Bible says communism will likewise be destroyed. All the dreams of men concerning world dominion and power were put into one dream, and this was the dream that the king of Babylon dreamed. These combined dreams were fashioned in the shape of a man, but God says that man's day will end and the Lord's day will begin. We believe the return of Christ is very near, and He will come like a rock to strike down all Gentile power and authority. He will rule the world with a rod of iron. This is the hope of this present generation.

We continue reading in Daniel 2:44-45: *"And in the days of these kings shall the God of heaven set up a kingdom, which shall never be destroyed: and the kingdom shall not be left to other people, but it shall break in pieces and consume all these kingdoms, and it shall stand for ever. Forasmuch as thou sawest that the stone was cut out of the mountain without hands, and that it brake in pieces the iron, the brass, the clay, the silver, and the gold; the great God hath made known to the king what shall come to pass hereafter: and the dream is certain, and the interpretation thereof sure."*

There were actually six parts to the Gentile empire

image of Nebuchadnezzar, because the fourth kingdom was divided into three parts. Five parts of the image have come to pass and been fulfilled just as Daniel said they would be. Only one part is left to be fulfilled. Even an unbeliever should be convinced that the remaining one-sixth will be fulfilled. The interpretation of the dream was sure.

Nebuchadnezzar saw the dream of man, a heaven on earth in which man himself is king, shattered. The lie with which Satan deceived Adam and Eve, that they would become as gods, will never be realized. The reason that man cannot build a stable political order, a just social order, and an acceptable moral standard, is that man himself is unstable, unjust, and immoral. As the old saying goes: "You can't make a silk purse out of a sow's ear." The whole is only a sum of all its parts. The Bible declares that all men have sinned and come short of the glory of God, and that there is none that doeth good, no not one. Therefore, to expect man of himself to establish a just and moral society on the earth is expecting the impossible. World War I was to make the world safe for democracy. It didn't. World War II was the war to end all wars. It didn't. The United Nations was supposed to bring peace on earth. It hasn't. The Great Society was supposed to erase poverty. It didn't. The industrial revolution was to build a heaven on earth. It didn't. Science was going to catapult man into a superhuman existence. It hasn't. And we could go on and on. The failure of man is due to his own sinful ineptitude, above which he cannot rise by himself. This is why God will send Jesus Christ back to save man for Himself.

Daniel tells us that in the days of the kings of the ten-nation kingdom that will rise up out of the Roman Empire at the end of the Gentile age, God will send Jesus Christ back. He is depicted as a rock appearing out of the sky to strike the Gentile image on its feet, and the entire monstrosity crumbles into dust and is blown away. But the rock becomes a huge mountain and fills the whole earth.

Notice first that this stone which strikes the image is cut out of a mountain without hands. In other words, man had nothing to do with it. It is extra-terrestrial in origin. And we know that Jesus Christ was born without the agent of a human father. He was conceived by the Holy Spirit and sent into the world by the Father. Such a stone was prophesied in Isaiah 28:16: *"Therefore thus saith the Lord God, Behold, I lay in Zion for a foundation a stone, a tried stone, a precious corner stone, a sure foundation: he that believeth shall not make haste."*

The kingdom which would be established upon this foundation is spoken of in Isaiah 32:1-2: *"Behold, a king shall reign in righteousness, and princes shall rule in judgment. And a man shall be as an hiding place from the wind, and a covert from the tempest; as rivers of water in a dry place, as the shadow of a great rock in a weary land."* The children of Israel looked forward to Christ as the blessed rock, and this is explained in 1 Corinthians 10:4: *"And did all drink the same spiritual drink: for they drank of that spiritual Rock that followed them: and that Rock was Christ."* In both Old and New Testaments, the Lord Jesus Christ of the Gentiles, the same as the Messiah of Israel, is spoken of as the sure foundation, a place of hiding in a weary storm, the spiritual rock which gives water of life, and the cornerstone of Israel. We read in Matthew 21:42, 44: *"Jesus saith unto them, Did ye never read in the scriptures, The stone which the builders rejected, the same is become the head of the corner: this is the Lord's doing, and it is marvellous in our eyes? . . . And whosoever shall fall on this stone shall be broken: but on whomsoever it shall fall, it will grind him to powder."*

Can there be any doubt left in anyone's mind that the rock which smote the image in the dream of Nebuchadnezzar, and literally ground it to powder, is none other than Jesus Christ? But let us not suppose that Jesus Christ is coming back to destroy the world. We read in Daniel 2:44 that He is coming back to establish a kingdom — to set up His own kingdom — a kingdom that will never be possessed or conquered by another, and a kingdom that will never pass away. We read about the establishing of His kingdom in Revelation 11:15: *". . . The kingdoms of this world are become the kingdoms of our Lord, and of his Christ; and he shall reign for ever and ever."*

Jesus Christ is not coming back to destroy the world; He is coming back to save the world from those who would destroy it (Rev. 11:18). He is coming back to replace all the rulers this world has ever known. He will be the King of kings, and He will rule the nations with an absolute rule after the order of Nebuchadnezzar — with the exception that all the laws of Jesus Christ will be just and righteous. Another view of what Daniel described to Nebuchadnezzar concerning the great and eternal King is provided in Matthew 25:31-32: *"When the Son of man shall come in his glory, and all the holy angels with him, then shall he sit upon the throne of his glory: And before him shall be gathered all nations: and he shall separate them one from another, as a shepherd divideth his sheep from the goats."*

The concluding four verses of chapter two state: *"Then the king Nebuchadnezzar fell upon his face, and worshipped Daniel, and commanded that they should offer an oblation and sweet odours unto him. The king answered unto Daniel, and said, Of a truth it is, that your God is a God of Gods, and a Lord of kings, and a revealer of secrets, seeing thou couldest reveal this secret. Then the king made Daniel a great man, and gave him many great gifts, and made him ruler over the whole province of Babylon, and chief of the governors over all the wise men of Babylon. Then Daniel requested of the king, and he set Shadrach, Meshach, and Abednego, over the affairs of the province of Babylon: but Daniel sat in the gate of the king"* (Dan. 2:46-49).

It is evident that Daniel made a great impression on the king of Babylon. He had done something that even the wisest men in the whole kingdom could not do. He confessed that Daniel's God was greater than all the gods of the Chaldeans. Daniel had been very careful to declare first to Nebuchadnezzar that the ability to recall the dream and the wisdom to interpret it, came not from within himself, but from the God of Heaven. This Nebuchadnezzar confessed, but still, he fell down and worshipped Daniel. This appears rather odd to those of us who worship God in spirit and in truth, but to Nebuchadnezzar it was evidently the normal and accepted thing to do. Heathen religions, like the religions of the Babylonians and Chaldeans, used idols as objects of worship. Such idols are necessary because their gods do not make their presence known through the spirit as the God whom we worship speaks to us through the Holy Spirit and leads us in the spirit according to His will. Therefore, in false religions, objects of worship such as idols are necessary so that the worshipper can feel that he is truly worshipping his god. And when Nebuchadnezzar fell down and worshipped Daniel, he was worshipping the only representation of this great God who had revealed the secret which was readily apparent. In his own way, he was attempting to direct worship to Daniel's God through the prophet himself. We believe that Daniel understood this, and this is why he accepted Nebuchadnezzar's worship in a heathen manner. This is in no way proper because we read in 1 Timothy 2:5: *"For there is one God, and one mediator between God and men, the man Christ Jesus."* Notice also that Nebuchadnezzar referred to Daniel's God as "your God," and not "my God."

Chapter Three

We begin our study of chapter three by reading the first seven verses: *"Nebuchadnezzar the king made an image of gold, whose height was threescore cubits, and the breadth thereof six cubits: he set it up in the plain of Dura, in the province of Babylon. Then Nebuchadnezzar the king sent to gather together the princes, the governors, and the captains, the judges, the treasurers, the counsellors, the sheriffs, and all the rulers of the provinces, to come to the dedication of the image which Nebuchadnezzar the king had set up. Then the princes, the governors, and captains, the judges, the treasurers, the counsellors, the sheriffs, and all the rulers of the provinces, were gathered together unto the dedication of the image that Nebuchadnezzar the king had set up; and they stood before the image that Nebuchadnezzar had set up. Then an herald cried aloud, To you it is commanded, O people, nations, and languages, That at what time ye hear the sound of the cornet, flute, harp, sackbut, psaltery, dulcimer, and all kinds of musick, ye fall down and worship the golden image that Nebuchadnezzar the king hath set up: And whoso falleth not down and worshippeth shall the same hour be cast into the midst of a burning fiery furnace. Therefore at that time, when all the people heard the sound of the cornet, flute, harp, sackbut, psaltery, and all kinds of musick, all the people, the nations, and the languages, fell down and worshipped the golden image that Nebuchadnezzar had set up"* (Dan. 3:1-7).

The Septuagint places the time of the dedication of this image of gold in the year 585 B.C., the same year that Nebuchadnezzar issued his third decree against Jerusalem for the people's stubborn attitude against complete sovereignty. It was at this time that the city was desecrated and the temple burned. This would place the event about seventeen years after Daniel had revealed to the king the secret of his dreams.

We note first that this image, or statue, that Nebuchadnezzar had constructed was sixty cubits high and six cubits wide, making it approximately ninety feet high and nine feet wide, and it was made of gold. There have been all kinds of theories about the construction of this idol. Some contend that it was only colored like gold, or that it was wood overlaid with gold, because that much gold would not have been available. However, we must remember that the armies of Babylon had ravaged all the nations of the Middle East, including Egypt, and had taken all the gold and silver back to Babylon. We should accept the scripture for what it says — that it was an image of gold. Of course, such a colossus made of the heaviest metal on earth would have weighed thousands of tons, and of necessity, would have had to be built upon a sturdy foundation. *Fausset's Bible Dictionary and Encyclopedia* states that Oppert found on the plains of Dura, southeast of Babylon, now called Duair, the pedestal on which a colossal statue once stood. So without doubt, the king of Babylon in the year 585 B.C. did dedicate a monstrous golden image. Either Nebuchadnezzar's heirs who followed him on the throne, or the Medo-Persians, cut the image up for the gold that was in it, leaving only the huge pedestal on which it stood.

We have every reason to believe that this was the same image which Nebuchadnezzar saw in his dream, with the exception that he made the entire image of gold, not inferior metals. We may indeed wonder if Nebuchadnezzar did not believe the interpretation that Daniel gave, but it is apparent that it was not so much that the king did not want to believe it, he simply did not approve of it. It did not strike his fancy that his kingdom would fall to another. He did not like the idea that his great wealth and power would fall to another. Kings never do. The more they accumulate, they more they become reluctant to face the reality of death. We read the words of Solomon in Ecclesiastes 2:18: *"Yea, I hated all my labour which I had taken under the sun: because I should leave it unto the man that shall be after me."*

The Chaldeans tickled Nebuchadnezzar's ears by always giving him their traditional greeting: "O king, live forever." This salutation was subsequently altered to: "Long live the king," because it became apparent over the centuries that kings, more or less, live threescore and ten years like everyone else. But

Nebuchadnezzar, like so many, was pleased by this deceiving flattery of these spiritists. He preferred fiction to fact. He certainly entertained the idea that he was divine and would live forever; so in his unrealities, he sought to alter God's plan. He would make the entire image of gold, the metal ascribed to himself and his empire; therefore, he would live forever and his kingdom would stand forever. He would prevent the God of Daniel from anointing His own King over the nations, and when the rock struck, his golden image would stand.

There have been many kings, politicians, philosophers, and generals who have tried to prevent the course of history as determined by God from continuing its natural course to its predestined conclusion. But no one to this date has been able to change the history of the world as presented in the image that Nebuchadnezzar saw in a dream. We read in Isaiah 14:24: *"The Lord of hosts hath sworn, saying, Surely as I have thought, so shall it come to pass: and as I have purposed, so shall it stand."*

Nebuchadnezzar commanded that any who would not worship the image should be killed, and we read that the Antichrist will do the same thing: *"And he had power to give life unto the image of the beast, that the image of the beast should both speak, and cause that as many as would not worship the image of the beast should be killed"* (Rev. 13:15). Six is the number of man, and there were two sixes in the dimensions of Nebuchadnezzar's image, indicating in symbolism his attempt to perpetuate man's day. However, the Antichrist will have three sixes in his number, as we read in Revelation 13:17-18: *"And that no man might buy or sell, save he that had the mark, or the name of the beast, or the number of his name. Here is wisdom. Let him that hath understanding count the number of the beast: for it is the number of a man; and his number is Six hundred threescore and six."*

Related to the building and worship of the image of Nebuchadnezzar was a plan to prevent the kingdom of Heaven being established here on earth under the sovereignty of Jesus Christ. This too will be the reason for the image of Antichrist. The Antichrist will try to force every person in the world to worship him, and demand blind obedience of the nations, even to the committing of all their armed forces to battle against the armies of Heaven when Christ returns (Rev. 16:14, 16; 19:11-21). This was the plan which the devil put into Nebuchadnezzar's head to prevent Christ's glorious reign over the earth, and the devil has not changed his plan because this was the best one that he could come up with. And this is why the Antichrist will again try to succeed where Nebuchadnezzar failed.

Next we notice that this mass idolatrous worship of the image by all the rulers of the nations, the judges, law enforcement officers, and petty politicians was to be accompanied by loud music of every type of musical instrument known at that time. It was a regular "rock festival." Now, why would Nebuchadnezzar accompany this anti-God mass with loud music?

Satan knows the power of music to stir the emotions of man and to deaden his natural senses. Loud and discordant music brings out the worst beastlike qualities in man and drives him on to godless pursuits and inhuman behavior. It is no wonder that Nebuchadnezzar used loud and harsh music at this worship service that was base and godless. And this is why we question the wisdom of using modern rock music in the worship service today.

When the image King Nebuchadnezzar had built was completed, the king sent invitations to every public official in all the Babylonian Empire to attend the unveiling. The invitation was quite simple. It stated that they could either attend or be cut into pieces. It would seem apparent that there were no rejections or excuses offered for not accepting.

Once they had all assembled, they were commanded to fall down and worship the image as a god. They could either fall down and worship the image or be taken the same hour and cast into a fiery furnace which the king had built a few hundred yards away from the image. The guests doubtless thought the king was going to prepare them a feast of barbeque, but they soon found out that unless they did what he wanted, they themselves would be the meat in the fire. Therefore, as the command was given and the band began to play, all the officials of the nations from Egypt to India fell down on their faces and worshipped the golden image. That is, with the exception of three men who remained standing. And with the thousands of the massive throng down on their faces in the dust, the three that remained standing stood out like a sore thumb.

"Wherefore at that time certain Chaldeans came near, and accused the Jews. They spake and said to the king Nebuchadnezzar, O king, live for ever. Thou, O king, hast made a decree, that every man that shall hear the sound of the cornet, flute, harp, sackbut, psaltery, and dulcimer, and all kinds of musick, shall fall down and worship the golden image: And whoso falleth not down and worshippeth, that he should be cast into the midst of a burning fiery furnace. There are certain Jews whom thou hast set over the affairs of the province of Babylon, Shadrach, Meshach, and Abednego; these men, O king, have not regarded thee: they serve not thy gods, nor worship the golden image which thou hast set up. Then Nebuchadnezzar in his rage and fury commanded to bring Shadrach, Meshach, and Abednego. Then they brought these men before the king. Nebuchadnezzar spake and said unto them, Is it true, O Shadrach, Meshach, and Abednego, do not ye serve my gods, nor worship the golden image which I have set up? Now if ye be ready that at what time ye hear the sound of the cornet, flute, harp, sackbut, psaltery, and dulcimer, and all kinds of musick, ye fall down and worship the image which I have made; well: but if ye worship not, ye shall be cast the same hour into the midst of a burning fiery furnace;

and who is that God that shall deliver you out of my hands? Shadrach, Meshach, and Abednego, answered and said to the king, O Nebuchadnezzar, we are not careful to answer thee in this matter. If it be so, our God whom we serve is able to deliver us from the burning fiery furnace, and he will deliver us out of thine hand, O king. But if not, be it known unto thee, O king, that we will not serve thy gods, nor worship the golden image which thou hast set up" (Dan. 3:8-17).

As part of Daniel's reward for revealing the king's dream and its interpretation, his three companions were appointed governors over the province of Babylon, which included the capital city. As the command was given to worship the image, the Chaldeans were keeping their eyes on these Jews. If the Jews remained true to their God, and failed to worship the image, then they would force the king to cast them into the furnace and the Chaldeans would claim their jobs. And as soon as the ceremony was over, the Chaldeans ran to the king. They reminded the king that according to his law, the three Hebrews must be thrown into the fiery furnace within the hour.

The king was absolutely furious, but he doubtless liked his three Jewish governors, and he said to them: "I'll tell you what I'm going to do. I'll have the band play my song one more time, and if you will fall down and worship the image, we will forget all about this first offense. But if you are still stubborn and refuse to worship the image, when the last note is played I will order the guards to overpower you and throw you into the furnace."

We notice in these last verses which we read that the musical portion of this false and idolatrous worship service is stressed twice again.

Music can be used to create any type of specific mental attitude that is desired. For example, in Germany before World War II radio stations played continually the harsh German military marches, and this type of music even invaded the churches. The young were caught up in the spirit of the music and were prepared to go out and fight the world if necessary. In 1936 Herr Baldur von Schirach, director of the youth program in Germany said:

"One cannot be a good German and at the same time deny God, but an avowal of faith in the eternal Germany is at the same time an avowal of faith in an eternal God. If we act as true Germans we act according to the laws of God. Whoever serves Adolph Hitler, the Fuhrer, serves Germany, and whoever serves Germany serves God."

Music had a role in creating this kind of blasphemy in the minds of German youth, and today music is being used to help destroy our country. It does make a difference what kind of music your children listen to; and it does make a difference what kind of music you have in your church. Music that is uplifting and soul-building is a gift of God and leads man to seek the One who will put a new song in his life. We read of the heavenly congregation in Revelation 5:8-9: "... *four and twenty elders fell down before the Lamb, having every one of them harps, and golden vials full of odours, which are the prayers of saints. And they sung a new song, saying, Thou art worthy to take the book, and to open the seals thereof: for thou wast slain, and hast redeemed us to God by thy blood out of every kindred, and tongue, and people, and nation.*"

The answer that these three young faithful Jews gave this heathen monarch is a classic, and it should be the Christian's answer to every temptation we are called to face. In essence, they told the king that his question about God being able to deliver them from the fiery furnace required no great wisdom or deliberation to answer, because the answer was self-evident. They assured the king that their God was able to deliver them from this horrible fate if He so desired, but perhaps it would be more for His glory should they die in the fire. Perhaps God would be glorified more in their death than in their life. There have been many instances where believers have been called upon to suffer martyrdom, and through their sacrifice, salvation has come to others by the spreading of the Gospel which was accomplished by their death. So the three faithful young Jews told the king that if it was God's will, they would be saved through the fire. If not, then they would die, but they would die serving God and not Nebuchadnezzar, or his false gods. They were assured that their God still lived, and whether they lived or whether they died, they belonged to Him.

In these days of cowardice and compromise, the moral and spiritual courage of Shadrach, Meshach, and Abednego can well serve as a pattern for God's people everywhere.

When Shadrach, Meshach, and Abednego refused to worship the image made by Nebuchadnezzar, the king went into a rage. We continue our study in Daniel 3:19-25: *"Then was Nebuchadnezzar full of fury, and the form of his visage was changed against Shadrach, Meshach, and Abednego: therefore, he spake, and commanded that they should heat the furnace one seven times more than it was wont to be heated. And he commanded the most mighty men that were in his army to bind Shadrach, Meshach, and Abednego, and to cast them into the burning fiery furnace. Then these men were bound in their coats, their hosen, and their hats, and their other garments, and were cast into the midst of the burning fiery furnace. Therefore because the king's commandment was urgent, and the furnace exceeding hot, the flame of the fire slew those men that took up Shadrach, Meshach, and Abednego. And these three men, Shadrach, Meshach, and Abednego, fell down bound into the midst of the burning fiery furnace. Then Nebuchadnezzar the king was astonied, and rose up in haste, and spake, and said unto his counsellors, Did not we cast three men bound into the midst of the fire? They answered and said unto the king, True, O king. He answered and said, Lo, I see four men loose,*

walking in the midst of the fire, and they have no hurt;
and the form of the fourth is like the Son of God."

The Babylonians used a particular type of smelting furnace. The furnace would be heated to a certain temperature, depending upon the type of metal they desired to melt. The metal would be thrown in at the top from a ramp, and the molten mass would be extracted at the bottom and poured into molds. It is evident that Nebuchadnezzar used this type of furnace to dispose of undesirables and those who questioned his absolute sovereignty over the empire. We read in Jeremiah 29:22: *"And of them shall be taken up a curse by all the captivity of Judah which are in Babylon, saying, The Lord make thee like Zedekiah and like Ahab, whom the king of Babylon roasted in the fire."* Nebuchadnezzar used the smelting furnace much like Hitler used his gas chambers — to dispose of the Jews.

The most common metal that was melted in these furnaces was iron, and in preparation for the disposal of the three Hebrews, Nebuchadnezzar commanded that the furnace be heated seven times hotter than it was normally heated. We would surmise that this meant that it was heated to a temperature seven times greater than is necessary to melt iron.

We read that the form of his visage was changed against the three Hebrews. Whereas he had formerly tried to persuade them to worship the image with reason and kindness, he now scowled and cursed them. He had actually humiliated himself in giving them a second chance, and in having spurned his mercy, he now vented his wrath upon them. He commanded his strongest guards to seize them immediately so there would be no chance of them getting away. Next, he instructed the guards to bind them with rope hand and foot. The king did not give them time to take off their clothing, and this was very expensive clothing indeed. The officials of Babylon were required to dress in a manner that would be pleasing to the king and make them proper ambassadors and representatives of Nebuchadnezzar. For such a high occasion to which they had been invited, they adorned themselves in their best formal wear. The Hebrew text explains the costliness of their fine and delicate silk garments.

As the guards approached the summit of the furnace, the flames were so high and so hot that they were overcome and burned to death. But Shadrach, Meshach, and Abednego slid on down the ramp into the raging inferno. In this particular type of furnace, there was a door on the bottom above the flames where the molten metal was extracted, and Nebuchadnezzar was squatting down on his haunches peering intently into the fire. As the three Hebrews hit the bottom he wanted to see them burn. This would be his revenge. However, we are informed that he was astonished to see the three Hebrews walking around in all their fine clothes. Not only did he see Shadrach, Meshach, and Abednego walking around in the fire, he saw another man — a fourth person.

According to the King James Version, Nebuchadnezzar identified the fourth person walking in the fire with the Hebrews as "the Son of God." The American Standard Version renders the same phrase as "a son of the gods." But regardless which version gives the more correct translation, it is quite evident that the fourth man was the Lord Jesus Christ. This was a preincarnate manifestation, a theophanic appearance of the Son of God. Jesus Christ said to the disciples: "Before Abraham was, I am." He was co-existent with the Father from before the foundation of the world. No man has seen God the Father at any time, but Jesus Christ His Son hath declared Him — not only in the New Testament, but in preincarnate appearances to the faithful in the Old Testament. It was the Lord God, God the Son, who walked with Adam in the Garden of Eden. It was God the Son who appeared to Joshua, and here in Daniel we find him walking with the faithful of Israel in the fiery furnace.

We read in 1 Peter 1:7: *"That the trial of your faith, being much more precious than of gold that perisheth, though it be tried with fire, might be found unto praise and honour and glory at the appearing of Jesus Christ."* The Lord God always walks with the faithful, even though the faithful are called to walk through the fire.

When Jesus revealed the glory that He had with the Father on the Mount of Transfiguration, His face shone as the sun and brilliant light radiated from His entire body. It was this glory which Nebuchadnezzar saw; thus, it is no small wonder that Nebuchadnezzar was greatly astonished.

We continue by reading Daniel 3:26-30: *"Then Nebuchadnezzar came near to the mouth of the burning fiery furnace, and spake, and said, Shadrach, Meshach, and Abednego, ye servants of the most high God, come forth, and come hither. Then Shadrach, Meshach, and Abednego, came forth of the midst of the fire. And the princes, governors, and captains, and the king's counsellors, being gathered together, saw these men, upon whose bodies the fire had no power, nor was an hair of their head singed, neither were their coats changed, nor the smell of fire had passed on them. Then Nebuchadnezzar spake, and said, Blessed be the God of Shadrach, Meshach, and Abednego, who hath sent his angel, and delivered his servants that trusted in him, and have changed the king's word, and yielded their bodies, that they might not serve nor worship any god, except their own God. Therefore, I make a decree, That every people, nation, and language, which speak any thing amiss against the God of Shadrach, Meshach, and Abednego, shall be cut in pieces, and their houses shall be made a dunghill: because there is no other God that can deliver after this sort. Then the king promoted Shadrach, Meshach, and Abednego, in the province of Babylon."*

We may wonder where Daniel was while all this was taking place, but the prophet does not even give a clue here in the third chapter. We know that Nebuchadnezzar respected and greatly feared Daniel because of his relationship with his God, whom the king recognized as a mighty and powerful God. It is quite possible that Nebuchadnezzer sent Daniel to another country on business in order to get him out of the province. Or, inasmuch as this event occurred at the time of the destruction of Jerusalem and the temple, it is possible that Daniel may have been at Jerusalem in order to try to save the Chronicles and the vessels and relics that remained after the burning of the temple. In any event, it seems quite apparent that Daniel was not in Babylon when this event occurred.

After the three Hebrews came out of the furnace, all the officials of the empire gathered around them, and they saw that though the ropes with which they were bound had been burned off, not a thread of their fine clothing had been singed or scorched. Their fine silk hose did not have a runner in them, and there was not even the smell of smoke on their garments.

Not only was the golden image a type of the image that Antichrist will build and command everyone to worship, but Shadrach, Meshach, and Abednego were a type of the faithful remnant of Israel who will be protected from the wrath of Antichrist and the tribulation fires for three and a half years just before the Lord returns. They will be preserved by the power of God, because like Shadrach, Meshach, and Abednego, they will refuse to worship the image of the beast in the temple, neither will they take his mark. Instead, they will place their faith in the God of

Abraham, Isaac, and Jacob. We read of this in Revelation 12:13-14.

For the second time, the power of the Omnipotent Creator was revealed to Nebuchadnezzar. The king was duly impressed again, and he swore there was no god like the Hebrew's God. He issued a decree that if any subject in the kingdom uttered blasphemy against this God, they would be cut into little pieces. But even yet, Nebuchadnezzar did not accept this God as his God. He still referred to the Almighty as the God of Shadrach, Meshach, and Abednego.

The overall object lesson of chapter three is that God's will and purpose for man and this earth cannot be changed by human will or power. Nebuchadnezzar, though it had been revealed to him the course of history by Daniel, still sought to change God's plan and purpose. But even a ninety-foot-high golden image was not enough, nor have all the armies of the world put together been enough. Napoleon, like Nebuchadnezzar, was the classic example of kings who seek to overstep their bounds even after being revealed the truth of God.

Victor Hugo described the events at the battle of Waterloo and he said that as Napoleon surveyed the field of battle, he said to his commanding officer: "We will put the infantry here, the calvary there, the artillery here. And at the end of the day England will be at the feet of France and Wellington will be prisoner of Napoleon." The commanding officer replied: "But we must not forget that man proposes but God disposes." With impatience the little emperor stuck out his chin and retorted angrily: "I want you to understand, sir, that Napoleon proposes and Napoleon disposes." Hugo concluded:

"From that moment Waterloo was lost, for God sent rain and hail so that the troops of Napoleon could not maneuver as he had planned, and on the night of battle it was Napoleon who was prisoner of Wellington, and France was at the feet of England."

We read in James 4:6: *". . . God resisteth the proud, but giveth grace unto the humble."*

Chapter Four

"Nebuchadnezzar the king, unto all people, nations, and languages, that dwell in all the earth: Peace be multiplied unto you. I thought it good to shew the signs and wonders that the high God hath wrought toward me. How great are his signs! and how mighty are his wonders! his kingdom is an everlasting kingdom, and his dominion is from generation to generation" (Dan. 4:1-3).

We notice a great change in the manner of speech of Nebuchadnezzar at the beginning of chapter four from the terminology he used at the conclusion of chapter three. At the close of chapter three he was threatening to cut anyone who challenged the power of God into little pieces, and this edict applied to every nation, race, and language. It was comparable to the edict of Emperor Constantine of Rome when he commanded that every citizen become a Christian. Something had happened between the close of chapter three and the beginning of chapter four which had made a new man out of Nebuchadnezzar, because he now speaks of all nations on earth from a position of peace. He declared: *"Peace be multiplied among you."* This is the terminology of a man who has received the grace of God. Paul, in all his epistles, greeted the churches in this manner. For example, we read in

Romans 1:7: *"To all that be in Rome, beloved of God, called to be saints: Grace to you and peace from God our Father, and the Lord Jesus Christ."*

Nebuchadnezzar pleads for an audience. He desires their attention, not because he wants them to do something for him, but rather because he has something good to tell them. He said: *"I thought it good to shew the wonders that God hath wrought toward me."* In other words, Nebuchadnezzar now had a testimony. The king was like the psalmist who declared: *"Come and hear, all ye that fear God, and I will declare what he hath done for my soul"* (Ps. 66:16). In chapter three it is revealed that Nebuchadnezzar built the golden image in a vain attempt to thwart God's plan to bring the rebel earth under His dominion and into His eternal kingdom, but here in chapter four the king confesses that the kingdom of God is an everlasting and eternal kingdom.

This testimony of the king of Babylon was issued in the year 562 B.C. The completion of the construction of the image of gold occurred in the year 585 B.C., thus about twenty-three years had elapsed between chapters three and four, and the events which led to the conversion of Nebuchadnezzar happened within this period. Beginning with Daniel 4:4, the king testifies to the world what these events were that led to his turning from idols and doctrines of devils to serve the living God. We continue and read Daniel 4:4-7: *"I Nebuchadnezzar was at rest in mine house, and flourishing in my palace: I saw a dream which made me afraid, and the thoughts upon my bed and the visions of my head troubled me. Therefore made I a decree to bring in all the wise men of Babylon before me, that they might make known unto me the interpretation of the dream. Then came in the magicians, the astrologers, the Chaldeans, and the soothsayers: and I told them the dream before them; but they did not make known the interpretation thereof."*

Nebuchadnezzar begins his testimony by relating an incident about a dream he had. At the time he dreamed this dream, he was at rest upon his throne, and he was living in great luxury in his great palace in mighty Babylon. He had conquered all the nations that could possibly threaten his empire, and the wealth of the world was pouring into his treasury.

Nebuchadnezzar, materially and politically speaking, was a self-satisfied man. But spiritually, he was greatly troubled. He had peace in his kingdom but there was no peace within his soul. He was financially wealthy but spiritually destitute. He believed there was a God because he had personally witnessed His mighty works, but there had been no personal acceptance of God as King of kings and Lord of lords.

We read that Nebuchadnezzar was troubled by a dream, and to help him solve his problem and ease his mind, he turned again to the magicians, the astrologers, the Chaldeans, and the soothsayers. He didn't send for Daniel, because the servant of God would have told him right off that he was troubled by a guilty conscience;

that he was living in sin and he needed the salvation that only God could give him. This was not what he wanted to hear.

Let us continue and read what happened after the astrologers and religious apostates failed to be of any help to the king in his despondent condition. *"But at the last Daniel came in before me, whose name was Belteshazzar, according to the name of my god, and in whom is the spirit of the holy gods: and before him I told the dream, saying, O Belteshazzar, master of the magicians, because I know that the spirit of the holy gods is in thee, and no secret troubleth thee, tell me the visions of my dream that I have seen, and the interpretation thereof. Thus were the visions of mine head in my bed; I saw, and behold a tree in the midst of the earth, and the height thereof was great. The tree grew, and was strong, and the height thereof reached unto heaven, and the sight thereof to the end of all the earth: The leaves thereof were fair, and the fruit thereof much, and in it was meat for all: the beasts of the field had shadow under it, and the fowls of the heaven dwelt in the boughs thereof, and all flesh was fed of it. I saw in the visions of my head upon my bed, and, behold, a watcher and an holy one came down from heaven; He cried aloud, and said thus, Hew down the tree, and cut off his branches, shake off his leaves, and scatter his fruit: let the beasts get away from under it, and the fowls from his branches: Nevertheless leave the stump of his roots in the earth, even with a band of iron and brass, in the tender grass*

*of the field; and let it be wet with the dew of heaven,
and let his portion be with the beasts in the grass of the
earth: Let his heart be changed from man's, and let a
beast's heart be given unto him; and let seven times
pass over him. This matter is by the decree of the
watchers, and the demand by the word of the holy
ones: to the intent that the living may know that the
most High ruleth in the kingdom of men, and giveth it
to whomsoever he will, and setteth up over it the
basest of men. This dream I king Nebuchadnezzar
have seen. Now thou, O Belteshazzar, declare the
interpretation thereof, forasmuch as all the wise men
of my kingdom are not able to make known unto me
the interpretation: but thou art able; for the spirit of
the holy gods is in thee"* (Dan. 4:8-18).

Nebuchadnezzar related in his testimony that
after his braintrust failed to come up with a satisfactory
explanation of his dream, God's representative entered
the scene. We can assume that Daniel, as the supervisor
of the wisemen, came in to check on their progress.
What he found was a very troubled king and the
magicians and astrologers standing around scratching
their heads. We must remember that up to this point,
the king was still an unconverted man, and he still
claimed Bel as his god, but inasmuch as Daniel's God
had given the prophet the interpretation of a previous
dream, he had confidence that He could do it again.
Therefore, Nebuchadnezzar committed the entire
matter to Daniel for a solution. The dream as the king
told it to Daniel was that he dreamed about a great

tree. This tree was so high it reached into the heavens, and wherever men lived on the face of the earth they could look up and see this tree. This tree was also a fruit tree that fed all the fowls of the air and the beasts of the field. Then one day a heavenly messenger from God came to inspect the tree, and he cut down the tree, but he left the stump and placed an iron band and a brass band around it. This was the dream that troubled the king's soul.

Forty years had passed since Nebuchadnezzar had the dream about the great image which represented the history of Gentile empires from Babylon to the kingdom of Heaven. The kingdom of Heaven is the kingdom which Christ will establish on earth when He comes the second time. Forty is the number of testing, and at the end of this period God considered Nebuchadnezzar again and found that in spite of the truth which had been revealed to him through Daniel, Shadrach, Meshach, and Abednego, the king continued to be a cruel and proud despot. So God spoke to him again in a dream and although he could not determine exactly what the dream meant, he considered it an evil omen. After the magicians, astrologers, and Chaldeans failed to interpret the dream, the king committed the matter to God's prophet, Daniel.

"Then Daniel, whose name was Belteshazzar, was astonied for one hour, and his thoughts troubled him. The king spake, and said, Belteshazzar, let not the dream, or the interpretation thereof, trouble thee. Belteshazzar answered and said, My lord, the dream

be to them that hate thee, and the interpretation thereof to thine enemies" (Dan. 4:19).

Daniel knew the interpretation of the dream immediately, but he was so stunned and shocked that he sat for a full hour without speaking. There are certain things that you cannot tell others. Even though it may be painful to tell a friend about the death of a loved one, or of a grievous financial loss, this is something that we can do because it is our duty. However, there are other types of news that are difficult to transmit. For example, it is difficult to tell a friend that he has dandruff, or possibly body odor, or that his wife is having an affair with another man. This is news which gentlemen find difficult to call to the attention of friends, and Daniel was certainly a gentleman. And the interpretation of this dream which Daniel received was of such an obnoxious and personal nature that he dreaded telling it to the king. So Daniel sat for one full hour with a frown on his face, and we would imagine that every few minutes he would cast a worried glance in the king's direction. Finally, the king could stand it no longer. The suspense was killing him. And so he finally said to Daniel: "Come on now. Nothing could be all that bad." And Daniel replied: "What is going to happen to you shouldn't happen to your worst enemy." We continue now from Nebuchadnezzar's testimony to find out what was really going to happen to him.

"The tree that thou sawest, which grew, and was strong, whose height reached unto the heaven, and the

sight thereof to all the earth; Whose leaves were fair, and the fruit thereof much, and in it was meat for all; under which the beasts of the field dwelt, and upon whose branches the fowls of the heaven had their habitation: It is thou, O king, that art grown and become strong: for thy greatness is grown, and reacheth unto heaven, and thy dominion to the end of the earth. And whereas the king saw a watcher and an holy one coming down from heaven, and saying, Hew the tree down, and destroy it; yet leave the stump of the roots thereof in the earth, even with a band of iron and brass, in the tender grass of the field; and let it be wet with the dew of heaven, and let his portion be with the beasts of the field, till seven times pass over him; This is the interpretation, O king, and this is the decree of the most High, which is come upon my lord the king: That they shall drive thee from men, and thy dwelling shall be with the beasts of the field, and they shall make thee to eat grass as oxen, and they shall wet thee with the dew of heaven, and seven times shall pass over thee, till thou know that the most High ruleth in the kingdom of men, and giveth it to whomsoever he will. And whereas they commanded to leave the stump of the tree roots; thy kingdom shall be sure unto thee, after that thou shalt have known that the heavens do rule. Wherefore, O king, let my counsel be acceptable unto thee, and break off thy sins by righteousness, and thine iniquities by shewing mercy to the poor; if it may be a lengthening of thy tranquility" (Dan. 4:20-27).

Throughout the Bible, trees are representative of nations, or if the king of the nation is an exceedingly strong monarch, then he too is represented in the symbolism. We read in Judges 9:8: *"The trees went forth on a time to anoint a king over them; and they said unto the olive tree, Reign thou over us."* And we read on down in this parable that the trees refer to nations, and there was one tree above all other trees, and this tall tree was the king. Nebuchadnezzar was the king of the nations in his time; therefore, it was readily apparent to Daniel that he was strong and his influence reached unto all the earth. There was no possible way for Daniel to soften the interpretation or for Nebuchadnezzar to misinterpret the meaning. The king was going to be cut down to the ground.

In verse twenty-three we read that a watcher and an holy one first came down from Heaven. The heaven spoken of here is the third Heaven where God's throne is located, and God's throne is the center of the kingdom of God, which includes the entire universe. So from the governmental center of the universe came two angelic beings to consider this great king who ruled over the great empire of Babylon. He had been witnessed to by God's ambassador here on earth, and he had been given forty years to change his ways. But instead of a more righteous and benevolent monarch, the watcher and the holy one found Nebuchadnezzar to be even more proud and still extending his power at the expense of the suffering masses. They concluded that the king had not submitted his authority to the will of God; there had been no change of heart; the time which God had given him to repent of his sins had expired; therefore, he was not only to be cut off from his kingdom, but to be cut off from the human race. God would give him the mind of a beast and he would eat grass in the field for seven years. The scripture says till seven times pass over him, and a "time" in the Hebrew was from one Passover to the next, or the period of one year. In Revelation 13:5 we read that the Antichrist will have great power over the nations of the world for forty-two months, or three and a half years. This period is the last half of the tribulation. This same period of three and a half years is also given in Revelation 12:14 as a time, times and half a time, and this would be three and a half years. Thus, it is evident that the Hebrew period of one time is the same as one year, and according to the prophetic interpretation of the king's dream, he was to become as a beast for seven years. From verse twenty-four it seems evident that God gave him the mind of an ox.

Both Daniel and Nebuchadnezzar were very emphatic as to the identity of the instrumentalities God used to carry out this particular judgment upon this haughty dictator. There were evidently two angelic personalities involved. One is called a watcher and one is referred to as a holy one, and both came from Heaven. We read in Daniel 4:17: *"This matter is by the decree of the watchers, and the demand by the word of the holy ones.. . ."* Thus, we understand that God has watchers and holy ones who assist Him in the administration of His universal government. Where the Scriptures identify Jesus Christ as the Great High Potentate, the King of kings, we should interpret them literally. He is the Father's anointed King over the kingdom of God. Where the Bible speaks of the kingdom of God, we should understand that this encompasses a literal kingdom. The capital of this universal system of government is a place of identification as the third Heaven, a literal planet. This is where the throne of God is located. The earth itself is a rebel planet within the kingdom of God. The human race itself, with the exception of the children of God among men, is in rebellion. They are living in sin, and the literal meaning of sin is to be in transgression against God, or to be in a state of rebellion against His will and authority. The kingdom of Heaven spoken of in the Bible refers to a future event when the King of kings, the Lord Jesus Christ, shall come and return this planet to the kingdom of God. He will place all rule and dominion under the authority of Heaven.

The veil of mystery is parted a little in the fourth chapter of Revelation to permit a glimpse into the legislative and administrative branches of the kingdom of God. We read in Revelation 4:2-11: ". . . *behold, a throne was set in heaven, and one sat on the throne. And he that sat was to look upon like a jasper and a sardine stone: and there was a rainbow round about the throne, in sight like unto an emerald. And round about the throne were four and twenty seats: and upon the seats I saw four and twenty elders sitting, clothed in white raiment; and they had on their heads crowns of gold. . . . Seven lamps of fire burning before the throne, which are the seven Spirits of God. . . . In the midst of the throne, and round about the throne, were four beasts full of eyes before and behind. And the first beast was like a lion, and the second beast like a calf, and the third beast had a face as a man, and the fourth beast was like a flying eagle"* (Rev. 4:2-7).

Notice that there are twenty-four seats around the throne of God. The seats relate to legislative positions. In our own nation when a political candidate runs for a position in Congress or the Senate, he is said to be trying for a seat in the legislative branch of our government. When he is subsequently defeated, he loses his seat. Therefore, it is easily determined that the twenty-four seats around the throne of God are high legislative positions within the kingdom of God. The elders are the holy ones. They are celestial princes as indicated by their golden crowns, and they hold dominion by delegated authority throughout the cosmos. It was by a decree of this high tribunal, composed of twenty-four elders, that Nebuchadnezzar was to be deprived of his kingdom and become as an ox. To understand the position of the holy ones and how the kingdom of God operates will bring out the complete meaning of Daniel 4:17: *"This matter is by the decree of the watchers, and the demand by the word of the holy ones: to the intent that the living may know that the most High ruleth in the kingdom of men, and giveth it to whomsoever he will, and setteth up over it the basest of men."*

Next, let us consider the position and sphere of authority of the watchers within the kingdom of God. Some commentaries contend that the original text indicates that the four beasts around the throne of God are living creatures. However, the Greek text calls these four beings *zoa*. The singular is *zoon*. *Zoa* is the root word for "zoology," indicating a collection of animals. Therefore, the King James Version renders an accurate translation in calling them beasts. It is self-evident that three of the living creatures are animal-like in appearance.

The traditional explanation is that the four beasts around the throne of God, be they creatures or beasts, represent the four-fold nature of Jesus Christ. The lion is symbolic of His kingship; the calf speaks of His humble servitude to mankind; the creature like a man relates to His humanity; and the flying eagle speaks of His divinity. Even though this symbolism may have significance, there is a more literal meaning. We read of the declaration of the four beasts and the holy ones in Revelation 4:11: *"Thou art worthy, O Lord, to receive glory and honor and power: for thou hast created all things, and for thy pleasure they are and were created."* The glory and honor and power which the four beasts ascribe to the Lord is the authority by which Christ will subdue the whole creation and redeem it from the curse of sin. The four beasts are described as being full of eyes and resting not day or night; they are vigilant and watching over the whole creation. The four watchers are described by John the Revelator as having six wings, identifying them as seraphim. The creature with the face of a lion is God's watcher over the wild animal kingdom; the seraphim with the face of an ox is the watcher over the domesticated animal kingdom; the seraphim with the face of an eagle is the watcher over the bird kingdom; and the one with the face of a man is the watcher over mankind. There is some scriptural evidence that Satan was a seraphim, an exalted watcher in the kingdom of God, before he rebelled against the authority of God. There is no mention made in the Scriptures of there being a watcher over the fish and reptile kingdom. *"Thou art of purer eyes than to behold evil, and canst not look on iniquity. . . . And makest men as the fishes of the sea, as the creeping things, that have no ruler over them"* (Hab. 1:13-14). The reason that there is no ruler over the cold-blooded animal kingdom could very well be that this was the position formerly held by Satan. This would also explain why Satan is called a snake and a red dragon, because there is a watcher who looks like a lion, one who looks like an ox, and one who looks like a bird. Satan looks like a serpent. When Satan appeared to Eve as a serpent, he appeared in his natural form.

Nebuchadnezzar's conduct was under constant surveillance by the watchers, and a report was made to the holy ones, and judgment was carried out according to a legislative decree.

We must never forget that kings and rulers are ministers of God in the area of human government. Even though a king or ruler may not believe in God or adhere to the ordinances of God, he still derives his authority to rule from God. We read in Romans 13:3-4: *"For rulers are not a terror to good works, but to the evil. . . . For he is the minister of God to thee for good. . . ."* There are ministers of God in the church and there are ministers of God in human government, and needless to say, there are apostates in both areas. Nebuchadnezzar had become an apostate king in that he ruled for his own power and glory rather than for the good of his people.

Let us continue and read Daniel 9:27: *"Wherefore, O king, let my counsel be acceptable unto thee, and break off thy sins by righteousness, and thine iniquities by shewing mercy to the poor; if it may be a lengthening of thy tranquility."*

Daniel was in a rather difficult position, and after he had finished the interpretation of the dream he tried to be as diplomatic as possible. He told the king that his advice was for him to quit his ungodly and wicked ways and be a good moral example to his people. Also, the king should begin showing more mercy to the poor — ease their tax burdens and grant them equal economic and political rights. The scripture does not say exactly how the king was to show mercy to the poor, but we should imagine that it would entail the things which have been mentioned. Daniel said that if the king would make these two specific changes, perhaps God would delay the judgment and he could continue his reign and his peace.

Did the king take Daniel's advice? We find the answer to that in the next five verses: *"All this came upon the king Nebuchadnezzar. At the end of twelve months he walked in the palace of the kingdom of Babylon. The king spake, and said, Is not this great Babylon, that I have built for the house of the kingdom by the might of my power, and for the honour of my majesty? While the word was in the king's mouth, there fell a voice from heaven, saying, O king Nebuchadnezzar, to thee it is spoken; The kingdom is departed from thee. And they shall drive thee from men, and thy dwelling shall be with the beasts of the field: they shall make thee to eat grass as oxen, and seven times shall pass over thee, until thou know that the most High ruleth in the kingdom of men, and giveth it to whomsoever he will."* (Dan. 4:28-32).

Let us keep in mind that this is Nebuchadnezzar's own testimony. He is telling all the people of the nations what happened to him, and how God had to break his stubborn pride before he would listen.

We know from archaeological discoveries that the palace of Nebuchadnezzar covered six square miles. Never had a king had such a palace. Twelve months after he had resolved to change his ways, he was walking about the palace, and its enormity and beauty began to overwhelm him. He said to himself: "Oh king, you are the greatest! Just look at this majestic edifice you have built with your own two hands!" In that moment of human weakness, the king forgot all about his resolutions. He forgot the lesson that God's servant had taught him — that all his glory, authority, and riches were by permission of the Lord.

We read in Ecclesiastes 8:11: *"Because sentence against an evil work is not executed speedily, therefore the heart of the sons of men is fully set in them to do evil."* The same truth is expressed in Proverbs 29:1: *"He, that being often reproved hardeneth his neck, shall suddenly be destroyed, and that without remedy."* We read in 2 Peter 3:9 that the Lord is longsuffering, and *"not willing that any should perish."* But the scripture does not say that there is no limit to the patience of the Lord. We read in Genesis 6:3: ". . . *My spirit shall not always strive with man. . . ."* Man can tempt God once too often. Nebuchadnezzar certainly did. We read about the result in Daniel 4:33: *"The same hour was the thing fulfilled upon Nebuchadnezzar: and he was driven from men, and did eat grass as oxen, and his body was wet with the dew of heaven, till his hairs were grown like eagles' feathers, and his nails like birds' claws."*

God took away the king's sanity and made him think that he was an ox. He left his beautiful and spacious palace, and went out into the fields of Babylon and ate grass with the cattle. He crawled around on all fours, and when night came he slept on the ground with the oxen.

This was one of the most solemn judgments that God ever brought against any man. He made a proud king behave like a dumb animal. He wore the same clothes for seven years; his hair became long and matted; his fingernails were long and dirty; and because he didn't bathe or wash, he was filthy, even worse than the animals with which he associated. We read in Proverbs 6:16-19: *"These six things doth the Lord hate: yea, seven are an abomination unto him: A proud look, a lying tongue, and hands that shed innocent blood. An heart that deviseth wicked imaginations, feet that be swift in running to mischief, A false witness that speaketh lies, and he that soweth discord among brethren."*

We continue and read Daniel 4:34-37: *"And at the end of the days I Nebuchadnezzar lifted up mine eyes unto heaven, and mine understanding returned unto me, and I blessed the most High, and I praised and honoured him that liveth for ever, whose dominion is an everlasting dominion, and his kingdom is from generation to generation: And all the inhabitants of the earth are reputed as nothing: and he doeth according to his will in the army of heaven, and among the inhabitants of the earth: and none can stay his hand, or say unto him, What doest thou? At the same time my reason returned unto me; and for the glory of my kingdom, mine honour and brightness returned unto me; and my counsellors and my lords sought unto me; and I was established in my kingdom, and excellent majesty was added unto me. Now I*

Nebuchadnezzar praise and extol and honour the King of heaven, all whose works are truth, and his ways judgment: and those that walk in pride he is able to abase."

When man in his own wisdom and pride looks downward and inward to himself, God gives him the mind of a beast because all beasts look down. Only when Nebuchadnezzar looked up did his sanity return. The lesson for us here is that the answer to all our problems lies in an upward direction. Nebuchadnezzar had received as much light and knowledge of God as any man could receive, yet he had to be brought low in judgment before he would believe and receive the God of whom Daniel witnessed. He was like most Americans today who have been preached to so much that they have become Gospel-hardened. But there is a limit to the patience and mercy of God. To this truth, Nebuchadnezzar testified to the world.

Chapter Five

As we study the book of Daniel, we should keep in mind that although it is a book of history, this is not its primary purpose. Even though it is historically correct in every detail, we could still inform ourselves of Babylonian history from secular records.

In many places, the book of Daniel is entertaining and humorous, because it depicts human weaknesses in real-life circumstances. We read in the second psalm that even God laughs at man in his folly. However, Daniel is not for our entertainment.

Daniel is also a book of psychology, because it reveals how men in their ambitions and greed think, act, and react. But Daniel is not for our psychological enlightenment.

Daniel is a book of God's revealed truth concerning a plan and program which He is working out for the world through men and nations. For over a thousand years before the flood, God dealt with the human race as one entity, and at the end of the Antediluvian age, the whole earth stood corrupt in His sight. Then, God called one man to establish a separate race that would testify to all men of His power and majesty and lead all mankind in peace and righteousness. The human race was thus divided into two parts — Jew and Gentile. We know the failure of

Israel to fulfill God's kingdom program from many books in the Old Testament. This nation failed miserably to live up to the ordinances of both the Abrahamic and Davidic covenants. After the Babylonian captivity, God did not expect them to fulfill the agreement made with Abraham or David. They did live on the land, but the land was under the control of Gentile powers. After Babylon, the throne of David was never restored. Israel, from Babylon to Christ, operated under the Levitic covenant. A temple and a high priest was all they had.

However, in Daniel God looks beyond Christ to the cutting off of Messiah. He looks beyond the dispensation of grace to the very end of the age, even to the conclusion of Gentile world government and the restoration of Israel as a nation. In Daniel God shows us how, in spite of Israel's apostasy and sin, He will bring to pass that which He has purposed — a kingdom here on earth in which Israel will be the head and not the tail. God saw fit to reveal through Daniel the characteristics, progress and culmination of the times of the Gentiles, and the coming again of Jesus Christ as King of kings and Lord of lords. The book of Daniel is a part of God's Word which is specifically written for our day. We read in Daniel 12:4: *"But thou, O Daniel, shut up the words, and seal the book, even to the time of the end: many shall run to and fro, and knowledge shall be increased."*

There are four pictures of the "times of the Gentiles" given in Daniel, and several specific illustrations which have end-time applications. The two specific descriptions of Gentile kingdoms that we have already studied are:

1. Nebuchadnezzar's dream which concerned the huge image. As explained by Daniel, the various components of this metallic monster represented four Gentile world empires.
2. Nebuchadnezzar's dream about a tree which reached up into the heavens.

Although this dream was prophetic of God's judgment against Nebuchadnezzar himself, it was a representation of the subduing of all Gentile nations under the authority of God at the end of the tribulation period. We notice that although Nebuchadnezzar had been given two specific warnings, he continued to claim all honor and glory unto himself and defy the God of Heaven. God gave him the mind of a beast and he was insane for seven years. During the seven-year tribulation period, the leaders of nations will act as mad men: they will defy God and accept the leadership of a ruler called the "beast." We read in Revelation 19:19: *"And I saw the beast, and the kings of the earth, and their armies, gathered together to make war against him that sat on the horse, and against his army."*

Nebuchadnezzar was not delivered from his madness until he looked up, and the nations will not be delivered from their delusions until they look up and see Jesus coming in the clouds of Heaven. We read in Luke 21:27-28: *"And then shall they see the Son of man coming in a cloud with power and great glory. And when these things begin to come to pass, then look up, and lift up your heads; for your redemption draweth nigh."* This is not a specific commandment to the church, because this scripture refers directly to the coming of Christ at the end of the tribulation. It has a greater meaning for the nations.

In the dream Nebuchadnezzar saw a band of iron and a band of brass placed around the stump of the tree. This indicated that although his insanity was a judgment from God, the Lord would not let him utterly destroy himself or his kingdom. During the tribulation, God will place bands upon the kings of the earth to keep them from utterly destroying the human race. We read in Psalm 2:2-4: *"The kings of the earth set themselves, and the rulers take counsel together, against the Lord, and against his anointed, saying, Let us break their bands asunder, and cast away their cords from us. He that sitteth in the heavens shall laugh: the Lord shall have them in derision."*

Thus, we see that Nebuchadnezzar's insane condition for seven years is representative in every detail of the state of the Gentile world during the seven-year tribulation period. His salvation is representative of the saving of the world from those who would destroy it (Rev. 11:18).

We continue our study and read Daniel 5:1:

"Belshazzar the king made a great feast to a thousand of his lords, and drank wine before the thousand."

As we begin chapter five, we notice first that a new king sits upon the throne of Babylon. Chapter four ends in 562 B.C.; chapter five is set in the year 536 B.C. Therefore, about twenty-three years elapsed between chapters four and five. Nebuchadnezzar died in 561 B.C., the year after he gave his testimony. Calvin doubted that he died a saved man; however, most theologians believe that he was saved. Without doubt, the king fulfilled his purpose in the plan of God for this world; therefore, he was taken from the scene.

Evil-merodach, Nebuchadnezzar's son, succeeded him on the throne (2 Kings 25:27-30). However, after a strong ruler dies, a period of political instability often follows. The reason for this political chaos is that a king or ruler is strong because he assumes all authority unto himself, and without men being prepared for the throne or rulership through delegated authority, turmoil results. There is usually a period of about ten years in which men in lesser positions contend for authority. After Nero's death, several men ascended to the throne within a very short time. In modern times, we remember what happened in Russia after the death of Stalin. Evil-merodach ruled over Babylon for only two years before Neriglissar, a son-in-law of Nebuchadnezzar, engineered the new king's assassination. But Neriglissar occupied the throne for only four years before he was killed. History indicates that he died in battle; however, it is very possible that his political enemies may have killed him to make it appear that he died at the hands of the enemy. After Neriglissar's death, his imbecile son Laborosoar-chad was placed upon the throne. He was beaten to death by Nabonidus in the year 555 B.C. Nabonidus was a political opportunist who married the widow of Neriglissar so that he might gain the throne.

These dull historical facts may not be of great interest to the average reader; however, we must refer to these changes within the government of Babylon in order to explain how Belshazzar was on the throne in the year 538 B.C. For many years critics of the Bible contended that Daniel was in error because there was no such man as Belshazzar mentioned in all of Babylonian history. According to secular records, Nabonidus was the last king of Babylon. More recent archaeological discoveries uncovered clay tablets on which the name Belshazzar as the son of Nabonidus is mentioned frequently. Jeremiah 27:7 would indicate that Belshazzar was probably the son of Evil-merodach, a direct heir to the throne and that he was adopted by Nabonidus in order to strengthen his claim to the throne and to keep the royal bloodline within his own family. Babylonian records indicate that Nabonidus thought himself to be quite a military strategist, and he was often away from the palace leading the armies of Babylon in battle. Belshazzar, the second ruler of the kingdom, was on the throne in Nabonidus' absence in the year 538 B.C. While the main body of the Babylonian army was on a foreign battle field, the

Medes and the Persians took advantage of the opportunity to lay siege to Babylon itself. These facts were substantiated by the archaeological discoveries made by Sir Henry Rawlingson in the year 1954 A.D. Thus, all God had to do to make foolish the wisdom of the wise was to put a spade into the hands of an Englishman and dig up some dirt.

At the beginning of chapter five we find Belshazzar on the throne of Babylon. His father, the king of Babylon, Nabonidus, was away in a distant province conducting a military campaign. His adopted son, Belshazzar, the second ruler of the kingdom, was serving as king in his absence. The Medes and the Persians, who were rebelling against Babylonian domination, took advantage of the situation to march on Babylon and lay siege to the city.

We may wonder why even a novice like Belshazzar would throw a party in time of national crisis. In the first place, he was probably advised by the defense minister that the city was absolutely secure, and there was no possible way for the enemy to bridge the defense network. However, military defenses are only as strong as the men who occupy their position.

In considering Babylon, we find that it was fifteen miles square, a city about the size of Houston, Dallas, Kansas City, or some other large American city. It had a population of one million people. Around the city was built a wall 350 feet high and 87 feet thick. Outside the inner wall, equally high, was a second wall. This second wall was one-half mile distant from the first wall, and between the two walls there was 30 square miles of rich soil. This area between the two walls was for just such an occasion as the siege by the Medes and the Persians. Even under siege, the city could produce enough food within its own walls to sustain the population. On top of the walls were 250 watch towers 450 feet high overall. On the outside of the wall was a deep water moat 30 feet wide. Water from the Euphrates kept the moat full at all times. Such a defense network around a city would present problems for a modern army, much less an army which had to attack with spears, bows and arrows, and scale walls by using ladders. So it is no small wonder that Belshazzar was proud and confident even during a period of military encirclement. All they had to do was to sit tight until Nabonidus returned with the main force of the Babylonian army.

We continue and read Daniel 5:2-4: "*Belshazzar, whiles he tasted the wine, commanded to bring the golden and silver vessels which his father Nebuchadnezzar had taken out of the temple which was in Jerusalem; that the king, and his princes, his wives, and his concubines, might drink therein. Then they brought the golden vessels that were taken out of the temple of the house of God which was at Jerusalem; and the king, and his princes, his wives, and his concubines, drank in them. They drank wine, and praised the gods of gold, and of silver, of brass, of iron, of wood, and of stone.*"

It is evident that Belshazzar took every advantage

of this opportunity to show off. Belshazzar was carried away with bravado and intemperance. He was going to throw a party the likes of which Babylon had never seen. The first thing that he did was to invite a thousand of the most important people in the city. As they were gathered together in the great meeting hall of the palace, Belshazzar commanded the servants to bring up from the wine cellar samples of the best wines. As the guests waited at attention, the king sampled the wine in order to select the very best to be served at his party.

After he had selected what he thought was the best wine, he commanded the servants to go to the national treasury and bring up the sacred vessels which were taken from the temple in Jerusalem. The wine from the cellar and the sacred vessels from the treasury arrived at the head table where Belshazzar was seated at the same time. Seated on one side were his wives, and on the other side the court prostitutes. The wine was poured into the sacred vessels, and Belshazzar arose from his seat and commanded silence from the crowd.

We do not know the reaction of the crowd as we are not told. Doubtless many remembered that Nebuchadnezzar revered the God of the Hebrews, and at one time had even issued a decree that if anyone blasphemed the name of the God of the Jews they would be cut up in little pieces. But here was Belshazzar openly defying Judah's God. The vessels used in the temple were dedicated to God's service, and they were all in some way used to tell God's redemptive story — the coming of Messiah and His atoning death for the sins of His people. All who desecrated the temple, the temple furniture, or the temple vessels, met with death. To defile the holy vessels constituted the utmost in blasphemy and sacrilege. But Belshazzar dared God to stop him from drinking wine out of the temple vessels, and he showed open contempt for the testimony of Nebuchadnezzar. So the reaction to the king's toast to the false gods of Babylon from the sacred vessels was probably mixed. Nevertheless, Belshazzar offered the toast and doubtless thought of himself as the life of the party. He had shown them how brave a king should be.

We continue now and read Daniel 5:5-9: *"In the same hour came forth fingers of a man's hand, and wrote over against the candlestick upon the plaster of the wall of the king's palace: and the king saw the part of the hand that wrote. Then the king's countenance was changed, and his thoughts troubled him, so that the joints of his loins were loosed, and his knees smote one against another. The king cried aloud to bring in the astrologers, the Chaldeans, and the soothsayers. And the king spake, and said to the wise men of Babylon, Whosoever shall read this writing, and shew me the interpretation thereof, shall be clothed with scarlet, and have a chain of gold about his neck, and shall be the third ruler in the kingdom. Then came in all the king's wise men: but they could not read the writing, nor make known to the king the interpretation thereof. Then was king Belshazzar greatly troubled, and his countenance was changed in him, and his lords were astonied."*

Alcohol and drugs provide moral cowards with the courage to perform foolish acts. The influence of strong drink deludes puny men into thinking they can defy the Almighty. Inasmuch as there is a prophetic significance for the Gentile nations at the end of the age in the fall of Babylon, we must conclude that this drunken and immoral party is quite symbolic of the degenerate condition of the Gentile world just before Christ returns.

This bragging little pipsqueak Belshazzar had challenged the God of Heaven, and to show His contempt for this little dictator, God showed him only His hand. God's little finger is more powerful than all the atheists and blasphemers in the world put together. We read in Psalm 8:3 that with His fingers, God created the heavens. We also read in Luke 11:20 that it was with one finger of God that Jesus cast out devils, and according to Exodus 8:19, with one finger God sent plagues upon Egypt that brought the proud and haughty pharaoh to his knees. And when the hand of God appeared before Belshazzar and began to write on the wall, the scripture says that the king's "countenance was changed." The drunken smile on his face was erased as fast as a word on a blackboard disappears when you rub an eraser across it. The alcohol deserted him in a second, and he became a terrorized coward.

"The king cried aloud to bring in the astrologers, the Chaldeans, and the soothsayers. And the king spake, and said to the wise men of Babylon, Whosoever shall read this writing, and shew me the interpretation thereof, shall be clothed with scarlet, and have a chain of gold about his neck, and shall be the third ruler in the kingdom. Then came in all the king's wise men: but they could not read the writing, nor make known to the king the interpretation thereof. Then was the king Belshazzar greatly troubled, and his countenance was changed in him, and his lords were astonied" (Dan. 5:7-9).

One minute the king of Babylon was boasting and bragging about his power and glory before the lords of the kingdom, and the next minute he becomes a crying, shaking, pleading, humiliating spectacle, and who did he call for in his fright? He called for the peddlers of demonism — the astrologers, the prognosticators, the spiritualists. The devil often takes advantage of men and women when they are afraid, because in their terror, they will accept help from any source.

In times of trouble, fear, and stress, there is only One who can help. He is the One mentioned by King David in the twenty-third psalm: *"The Lord is my shepherd; I shall not want. He maketh me to lie down in green pastures: he leadeth me beside the still waters. He restoreth my soul: he leadeth me in the paths of righteousness for his name's sake. Yea, though I walk through the valley of the shadow of death, I will fear no evil: for thou art with me; thy rod and thy staff they comfort me"* (Ps. 23:1-4).

Thus, we see that the devil has never changed his method of operations. He always has his agents in the right place at the right time — to ensnare the scared, the weak, and the ignorant.

Belshazzar promised a purple coat, a solid gold chain, and the office of third ruler in the kingdom to anyone who could tell him what the writing said. He did not offer to make the one who could interpret the writing the second ruler because that was his job. But as we would expect, the devil's men could not read the writing on the wall because it was written by God.

We continue and read Daniel 5:10-12: *"Now the queen by reason of the words of the king and his lords came into the banquet house: and the queen spake and said, O king, live for ever: let not thy thoughts trouble thee, nor let thy countenance be changed: There is a man in thy kingdom, in whom is the spirit of the holy gods; and in the days of thy father light and understanding and wisdom, like the wisdom of the gods, was found in him; whom the king Nebuchad-nezzar thy father, the king, I say, thy father, made master of the magicians, astrologers, Chaldeans, and soothsayers; Forasmuch as an excellent spirit, and knowledge, and understanding, interpreting of dreams, and shewing of hard sentences, and dissolving of doubts, were found in the same Daniel, whom the king named Belteshazzar: now let Daniel be called, and he will shew the interpretation."*

It is thought by many that the queen mentioned here was not the wife of Belshazzar, but the queen mother, the wife of Nebuchadnezzar or Evil-merodach. In any event, she was evidently a wise woman. The testimony of Nebuchadnezzar had doubtless bore much fruit among the members of the court. She may not have been at this wild party by choice, or it could be that Belshazzar didn't invite her.

The queen in her chamber had been listening to the drunken brawl and suddenly everything got as quiet as the lull before the storm. Then she could hear the king's voice trembling with fear and begging someone to please interpret the writing on the wall. It was her duty to help the king if she could; therefore, she left her chamber and went into the banquet house. She informed the king that there was a man in the kingdom who could help him. He had helped his father in similar situations, and she believed he could do the same for him. Belshazzar was Nebuchadnezzar's grandson. There is no word in the Hebrew for grandfather. All male descendants from a singular head are sons, and the head is father, regardless of whether the head is a father, grandfather, great-grandfather, etc. In his present state, Belshazzar was king. Belshazzar either did not know, or had forgotten about Daniel. Since the death of Nebuchadnezzar, it appears that Daniel had slipped into obscurity. At least, his counsel had become unpopular in the higher echelons of the Babylon government.

We continue and read Daniel 5:13-17: *"Then was*

Daniel brought in before the king. And the king spake and said unto Daniel, Art thou that Daniel, which art of the children of the captivity of Judah, whom the king my father brought out of Jewry? I have even heard of thee, that the spirit of the gods is in thee, and that light and understanding and excellent wisdom is found in thee. And now the wise men, the astrologers, have been brought in before me, that they should read this writing, and make known unto me the interpretation thereof: but they could not shew the interpretation of the thing: And I have heard of thee, that thou canst make interpretations, and dissolve doubts: now if thou canst read the writing, and make known to me the interpretation thereof, thou shalt be clothed with scarlet, and have a chain of gold about thy neck, and shalt be the third ruler in the kingdom. Then Daniel answered and said before the king, Let thy gifts be to thyself, and give thy rewards to another: yet I will read the writing unto the king, and make known to him the interpretation."

Daniel was now an old man of eighty-three years. He had already received from Nebuchadnezzar all the honor the Babylonian empire could bestow upon him.

When Daniel appeared in the door to the banquet hall, the one thousand lords and their ladies were anxiously awaiting his arrival. God's prophet doubtless took careful note of the holy vessels from the temple that had been desecrated by the king's wine. As he passed through the door, the king arose from his royal chair, and with outstretched arms and a big smile on his face, he said: "So this is Daniel! I have heard so many great and wonderful things about you. I have heard that you are the best wise man in all Babylon, and I'll tell you what I am going to do. Tell the interpretation of the writing on the wall, and I will have my tailor fit you with a bright new purple coat. I'll give you a brand-new gold chain to wear around your neck. And, I'll make you the third ruler over all the kingdom of Babylon. You will have your own palace, well-stocked with maids and servants."

Perhaps a less godly or experienced man would have been taken in by all this fakery, flattery, and bribery. But not Daniel. He was in no mood to indulge in such a charleton as Belshazzar. He didn't even give the king the usual royal greeting. In fact, he didn't even greet him at all. He walked up to the king and looked him straight in the eye. The scripture says that he was before the king; and we can imagine Daniel said: "King, in the first place, I don't want your gifts and neither do I want to be even the first ruler of Babylon. Give your gifts to someone else." To refuse to accept the king's gifts was in itself a grievous insult, and on any other occasion, would have meant Daniel's head. But Daniel continued and said: "Even though I don't want anything from you, or any part of you, I will tell you the interpretation of the writing on the wall. But before I do, I am going to preach you a sermon." And right there in the banquet hall in the middle of the night Daniel preached this insolent snob a sermon.

Daniel's sermon to the king of Babylon is recorded in Daniel 5:18-24: *"O thou king, the most high God gave Nebuchadnezzar thy father a kingdom, and majesty, and glory, and honour: And for the majesty that he gave him, all people, nations, and languages, trembled and feared before him: whom he would he slew; and whom he would he kept alive; and whom he would he set up; and whom he would he put down. But when his heart was lifted up, and his mind hardened in pride, he was deposed from his kingly throne, and they took his glory from him: And he was driven from the sons of men; and his heart was made like the beasts, and his dwelling was with the wild asses: they fed him with grass like oxen, and his body was wet with the dew of heaven; till he knew that the most high God ruled in the kingdom of men, and that he appointeth over it whomsoever he will. And thou his son, O Belshazzar, hast not humbled thine heart, though thou knewest all this; But hast lifted up thyself against the Lord of heaven; and they have brought the vessels of his house before thee, and thou, and thy lords, thy wives, and thy concubines, have drunk wine in them; and thou hast praised the gods of silver, and gold, of brass, iron, wood, and stone, which see not, nor hear, nor know: and the God in whose hand thy breath is, and whose are all thy ways, hast thou not glorified: Then was the part of the hand sent from him; and this writing was written."*

Daniel had a duty to perform. God commanded his servants to expose and condemn sin regardless whether sin is committed by the lowest citizen or the national head of state. Samuel looked Saul straight in the eyes and said: *". . . Thou hast done foolishly: thou hast not kept the commandment of the Lord thy God . . ."* (1 Sam. 13:13). Nathan rebuked David after the king had killed Uriah for his wife. We read in 2 Samuel 12:9: *". . . thou despised the commandment of the Lord, to do evil in his sight. . . ."* Elijah called upon Ahab to give an account of his sins; John the Baptist exposed the sin of Herod, and we could give many other examples. Ministers of God do have a duty to challenge sin in high places; because God does rule in the affairs of men and of nations, and He sets up and He tears down. Nations suffer not only for the sins of the people, but also for the sins of their leaders. The entire nation of Babylon was about to suffer for the sins and blasphemy of its king.

Daniel pointed his finger at Belshazzar and reminded him that his grandfather was a great man. He ruled with an iron hand and God gave him a mighty empire. But because he became proud and failed to give God the glory or observe God's ordinances for human government, Nebuchadnezzar was cut down to the ground and given the mind of an ox until he was humbled and acknowledged the sovereignty of God. Daniel reminded the king of the truth found in Romans 9:21: *"Hath not the potter power over the clay. . . ."* God's prophet told the king that he knew what happened to his grandfather when he failed to bend to the authority of the Creator, and now he was lifting himself against the same Lord of Heaven. He was defying the Lord by corrupting His holy vessels with contaminated wine and the lips of court prostitutes. This same God which Belshazzar defied was the One who held the king's own breath in his hand and He could snuff it out as easy as one would blow out a candle. Let us read again this admonition which Daniel gave to Belshazzar, because it is a truth that we all need to keep constantly before us: "... *God in whose hand thy breath is, and whose are all thy ways, has thou not glorified."*

Belshazzar did not challenge God ignorantly. He did it knowingly and proudly. He rejected the Divine Almighty for the gods of affluence — the gods of gold, silver, brass, iron, wood, and stone. They were the children of Bel — the lesser Babylonian deities. Belshazzar is numbered among those spoken of in Romans 1:28: *"And even as they did not like to retain God in their knowledge, God gave them over to a reprobate mind. ..."* After exposing to the king the error of his sinful ways, and then pointing him to God as the One who held his very life in His hands, Daniel proceeded to tell the king what he wanted to know.

Reading next Daniel 5:25-31: *"And this is the writing that was written, Mene, Mene, Tekel, Upharsin. This is the interpretation of the thing: Mene; God hath numbered thy kingdom, and finished it. Tekel; Thou art weighed in the balances, and art found wanting. Peres; Thy kingdom is divided, and given to the Medes and Persians. Then commanded Belshazzar, and they clothed Daniel with scarlet, and put a chain of gold about his neck, and made a proclamation concerning him, that he should be the third ruler in the kingdom. In that night was Belshazzar the king of the Chaldeans slain. And Darius the Median took the kingdom, being about threescore and two years old."*

The writing on the wall was in Aramaic and may have been arranged in acrostic style as it is shown in the Talmud. Rather than reading from left to right or from right to left, it should have been read from the top to the bottom. But Daniel had no trouble at all in either reading it or decoding its message.

Mene: *Mene* in the Aramaic means "number." To double wording (Mene, Mene,) meant that God had numbered the years of the Babylonian Empire and that the number had now expired. In other words, Daniel told Belshazzar that his number was up. The prophet Jeremiah prophesied that Israel would be held captive by Babylon for a generation — seventy full years. The appearance of Daniel before Belshazzar came at the end of the seventieth year of Babylonian captivity.

Tekel: The next word (*Tekel*) means "to weigh," to test the net worth of gold, silver, or other commodities according to a weight standard. God's scales or balances weigh people, rulers, and nations. We read in

1 Samuel 2:3: *". . . the Lord is a God of knowledge, and by him actions are weighed."* Job 31:6: *"Let me be weighed in an even balance, that God may know mine integrity."* Psalm 62:9: *". . . men of high degree are a lie: to be laid in the balance. . . ."* Men's balances may swing like a pendulum to determine the innocence or guilt of the accused, but God's balances are sure and accurate because known unto Him are all our ways, our debts, and our thoughts. God weighed Belshazzar, and though he may have made a good dishwasher, a stable keeper, or a bartender, a king he was not. He was not even worth saving. The people of Babylon were guilty with him in his folly, because they approved of the moral standards. In other words, they liked the king because he did the things which they also like to do.

Upharsin: Commentary on the Aramaic text indicates that *Upharsin* is a combination of two words — *peras* meaning "to break or divide," and *pharsin* meaning the "Persians." Thus, the interpretation given by Daniel: *"The kingdom is divided, and given to the Medes and Persians."*

Whether there was any true repentance on Belshazzar's part in the last hours of his life, we are not told. The only thing to his credit is that even though he must have known he did not have long to live, he fulfilled his kingly duty and kept his word. The king's word was law, and the king himself, above all others, must be true to his word.

Although Daniel had spurned Belshazzar's offer of gifts and honor, the king's integrity must be upheld. Therefore, Daniel was forced to accept a scarlet robe, a gold chain, and the position of third ruler of the kingdom.

Belshazzar and his generals thought that Babylon was invincible. However, the Medes and the Persians had their spies in the city. It must have been known that on this particular night all the high officers in the army and governmental officials would be at the king's party. The immoral conditions of Babylon had lessened their national vigilance. The Medo-Persian army was divided into three main forces. One force went upstream and diverted the channel of the Euphrates River. A second force made itself ready to advance on the city from the north. The third force was to come from the south. As the water level fell, the two armies marched from opposite directions up the river bed and entered the city in the early morning hours before daylight. The king and his military high command were slain. The city experienced little battle damage, and the conquest was so swift and complete, history records that it was several days before many citizens knew that there had been a change in the government. Like an overripe fruit, it fell into the hands of its conquerors. Its fall was not caused by the lack of military power, but rather because of apostasy and gross immorality.

Chapter Six

We read in Daniel 5:31 that at the fall of Babylon, Belshazzar was killed and Darius the Median took over the kingdom. However, the commander in charge of the Medo-Persian army, and the man who engineered the capture of Babylon, was the Persian general Cyrus. This was prophesied by Isaiah one hundred seventy-five years prior to this great historical event.

Cyrus was not a believer in God when he lay siege to Babylon, and he did not even know that he was mentioned in prophecy and destined to become ruler of the world. Cyrus could have easily become king of the new world empire had he so desired, but he deferred to Darius of the Medes. The word *darius* is simply a Persian title for ruler, king, or caesar. It is thought by historians that Darius of the Medes was Cyrus' father-in-law, who was the king of Media. Darius was getting along in years, sixty-two years old, and he was without a male heir. Therefore, Cyrus gave him the honor of ruling over the Medo-Persian Empire for two years. This was doubtless the arrangement to which both men agreed. Darius was not a strong king, and he ruled through delegated authority as we read in Daniel 6:1-2: *"It pleased Darius to set over the kingdom an hundred and twenty princes, which should be over the whole kingdom; And over these three presidents; of whom Daniel was first; that the princes might give accounts unto them, and the king should have no damage."*

These two verses describe the nature of the government of the Medo-Persian Empire. It was not the absolute monarchy that Babylon was. It was as silver compared to gold, and thus we see the golden head of Babylon replaced by the two-part silver empire that comprised the two arms of the image that Nebuchadnezzar saw in a dream. The government was administered through one hundred twenty members of the royal households of Media and Persia. Each prince ruled over a province, and then a president was appointed over forty of the provinces, or states as we call them in our own country. The job of the president was to pass on to the princes the governmental policy and orders of the king. He was also to see that the princes were diligent and orderly in their duties. The government of the Medo-Persian Empire was actually a monarchal-republican form of government. The agreement between Darius and Cyrus and the institution of this particular type of government administration was reported by Xenophon the historian.

Daniel had endured through six Babylonian kings, a most remarkable accomplishment. And when Belshazzar made Daniel the third ruler of the kingdom on the night of his own death, he was really not doing Daniel any favor. In fact, it would have seemed to serve as Daniel's death warrant. Even though the Medes and Persians were more democratic in the administration of government, this does not mean they were less ruthless in dealing with political enemies than the Babylonians. History records that Cyrus crucified three thousand Babylonian political enemies. Doubtless all of the one thousand lords of Babylon who attended Belshazzar's party were included in this number who were executed. We would certainly expect Daniel, the third ruler of Babylon, to have been included in this execution of high political Babylonian officials; however, not only was he spared, but he was made one of the three presidents of the empire. Reading next Daniel 6:3: *"Then this Daniel was preferred above the presidents and princes, because an excellent spirit was in him; and the king thought to set him over the whole realm."*

Here we find that Daniel was so highly regarded by Darius, he was preferred above the other two presidents, and the new ruler consulted Daniel first about all important governmental matters relating to both domestic and foreign affairs. Daniel was experienced (he had been connected with Babylonian affairs for over sixty years); he knew who could be trusted and who could not be trusted; he knew Babylon like the back of his hand; and Darius found that he owed no particular allegiance to Babylon and that he could be trusted. He was certainly a valuable man to have around.

As Daniel served in this high administrative position, he arose in favor because of the excellent spirit that was in him. He was faithful to see that no damage came to the king.

Behind Daniel's rise to power in the new government we see the hand of God. God had said that after the fall of Babylon, Cyrus would allow a remnant to return to Jerusalem and rebuild the temple and the city. God was still using Daniel to carry out His plan and program for the world. Daniel was to witness to the new rulers of the kingdom and prepare their hearts to deal kindly with the Jews and let them return. Even in his mid-eighties, God was still keeping Daniel active in His service.

With the institution of Daniel in the government of the Medo-Persian Empire, we witness the fall of one empire and the rise of another. Now, the question often arises: "Will Babylon ever rise again?" As we have brought out many times, the city of Babylon will be rebuilt. The Babylonian system will spread to all Gentile nations, the foremost of which is our own country, but the city itself will be rebuilt on its old site.

We are well aware that Dr. C.I. Scofield and others said that Babylon would never rise again. Dr. Scofield was very good on doctrine, but he was weak on some major points in prophecy. Perhaps the greatest prophetic scholar of this century so far was Rev. Clarence Larkin. More and more, prophetic fulfillments are proving that he was correct in his prophetic dissertations. In 1929, over sixty years ago, Dr. Larkin wrote concerning the rebuilding of Babylon:

"That the ancient city of Babylon restored is

to play an important part in the startling events of the last days of this dispensation is very clear. This is seen from what is said of it in the seventeenth and eighteenth chapters of the book of Revelation. At first sight the two chapters, which contain some things in common, are difficult to reconcile, but when we get the 'key,' the reconciliation is easy. The seventeenth chapter speaks of a 'woman' called 'mystery, Babylon the Great, the Mother of Harlots and Abominations of the Earth.' The eighteenth chapter speaks of a city, a literal city, called 'Babylon the Great.' That the woman and the city do not symbolize the same thing is clear, for what is said of the woman does not apply to the city, and what is said of the city does not apply to a woman. The woman is destroyed by the ten kings, while the 'kings of the earth' in the next chapter 'bewail and lament the destruction of the city,' which is not destroyed by them, but by a mighty earthquake and fire. Again, the woman is destroyed three and a half years before the city; and the fact that the first verse of chapter eighteen says, 'After these things,' that is after the destruction of the woman . . . shows that the woman and the city are not one and the same. That the two chapters refer to different things is further verified by the fact that they are announced by one of the vial angels, while those spoken of in chapter eighteen are announced by 'another' angel, probably the second angel messenger. If the mystical Babylon was destroyed in chapter seventeen, she cannot appear in chapter eighteen; therefore the city described in chapter eighteen must be a literal city called Babylon. As there is no city of that name on earth today, the reference must be to some future city of Babylon. The city of Babylon is so intimately connected with the history of God's people, the Jews, that the Scriptures have much to say about it. A large part of the book of Daniel has to do with it; and it is mentioned in twelve other books of the Old Testament, and in four of the New Testament. And that Daniel is proven by the fact that the city of Babylon is again spoken of in it, and its prominence in the affairs of the world at the 'end time.'"

The objection which Dr. Scofield and others have had to the literal rebuilding of Babylon is that it was prophesied in Isaiah and Jeremiah that Babylon would be destroyed, never to rise again. But if we carefully read these prophecies in the Old Testament, we find that some refer to the fall of Babylon as described in chapter five, while others look forward to the end of the age to the destruction of the last Babylon. For example, *"And Babylon, the glory of kingdoms, the beauty of the Chaldees' excellency, shall be as when God overthrew Sodom and Gomorrah. It shall never be inhabited, neither shall it be dwelt in from generation to generation: neither shall the Arabian pitch tent there; neither shall the shepherds make their fold there"* (Isa. 13:19-2).

There is no way this prophecy could have been fulfilled at the fall of Babylon when Belshazzar was king. Sodom and Gomorrah were destroyed by fire in an hour, and so will the last Babylon be destroyed in an hour (Rev. 18:19). The Medes and Persians captured Babylon without any physical destruction. And the Arabs have pitched their tents there and fed their sheep there ever since. We read in Jeremiah 51:26: *"And they shall not take of thee a stone for a corner, nor a stone for foundations; but thou shalt be desolate for ever, saith the Lord."*

One can go to the site of the old Babylon and still find buildings made out of the ruins of the first Babylon. There has always been a city of some size on the site of old Babylon. Yet, we read in Revelation that when the last Babylon is destroyed, there will be nothing left but a hole in the ground, just as prophesied by Isaiah and Jeremiah. Only the birds will be able to nest on the sides of the cliffs.

We were in Babylon and with our own eyes saw workmen busy reconstructing many of the buildings, temples, and wall of the city.

We continue and read Daniel 6:4-9: *"Then the presidents and princes sought to find occasion against Daniel concerning the kingdom; but they could find none occasion nor fault; forasmuch as he was faithful, neither was there any error or fault found in him. Then said these men, We shall not find any occasion against this Daniel, except we find it against him concerning the law of his God. Then these presidents and princes assembled together to the king, and said thus unto him, King Darius, live for ever. All the presidents of the kingdom, the governors, and the princes, the counsellors, and the captains, have consulted together to establish a royal statute, and to make a firm decree, that whosoever shall ask a petition of any God or man for thirty days, save of thee, O king, he shall be cast into the den of lions. Now, O king, establish the decree, and sign the writing, that it be not changed, according to the law of the Medes and Persians, which altereth not. Wherefore king Darius signed the writing and the decree."*

Greedy and incompetent employees always hate a dedicated and efficient employee because the good worker will show them up for the lazy loafers that they are. The other two presidents and the rulers over the provinces hated Daniel because he expected the high degree of performance which he himself gave to the king. First, they tried to uncover errors in his work, but they couldn't find a single one. Next, they tried to find a flaw in his character, but he was above reproach.

The leaders of this conspiracy against Daniel went to the king with what appeared to be a patriotic project. They told the king that in order to strengthen his hold over the Babylonians, all the presidents, all the governors, all the princes, all the counsellors, and all the captains of the army had decided upon a plan.

This plan was to be in the form of a royal decree whereby no man in all the kingdom would make a petition, request, or ask a favor of any God or any man, other than the king, for thirty days. It was to be "King Darius Month." They said: "We have all agreed that for the good of the country, you should make this decree. We have got to show these Babylonians who is boss."

Darius was not another Nebuchadnezzar. We see little evidence of personal pride in the decision he made. It was his duty to consider carefully the advice of the governors, princes, and presidents. He honestly thought that this advice had been approved by his top president, Daniel, because the conspirators told him that **all** the presidents were included in the consultations.

Of course, they lied; but even so, Darius could not reverse the decree once it was made. According to the Divine Right of Kings rule under which all the old monarchists operated, the king could do no wrong. Even should the king sentence a man to death for a crime, and it was later proven that the man was innocent, the man would have to be executed. The king could never admit that he had made an error. Therefore, these conspirators were very insistent that their scheme be put in the form of an unbreakable royal statute rather than the form of a memorandum or resolution. Once it was signed by the king it became the supreme law of the land and even Darius himself could not reverse it.

The second phase of the plot called for a twenty-four-hour stakeout on Daniel's apartment. All they had to do was catch Daniel just once asking God to do something for him or his people, and then they could get this troublemaker fed to the lions.

We continue and read Daniel 6:10-13: *"Now when Daniel knew that the writing was signed, he went into his house; and his windows being open in his chamber toward Jerusalem, he kneeled upon his knees three times a day, and prayed, and gave thanks before his God, as he did aforetime. Then these men assembled, and found Daniel praying and making supplications before his God. Then they came near, and spake before the king concerning the king's decree; Hast thou not signed a decree, that every man that shall ask a petition of any God or man within thirty days, save of thee, O king, shall be cast into the den of lions? The king answered and said, The thing is true, according to the law of the Medes and Persians, which altereth not. Then answered they and said before the king, That Daniel, which is of the children of the captivity of Judah, regardeth not thee, O king, nor the decree that thou hast signed, but maketh his petition three times a day."*

God made a definite promise to the children of Israel in 1 Chronicles and 2 Kings. It was at the time that Solomon dedicated the temple, and the theocratic head of the nation, speaking with authority from God, told the children of Israel that if at any future time they should sin and God turn His face from them and allow them to be carried captive into foreign lands, they should do certain things. First, they should forsake their sins and return to God with all their hearts. Next, from the land of their captivity, they should turn toward the land of Israel and pray —pray even in the direction of the Lord's house, the temple. If they repented and prayed earnestly and diligently, seeking God's forgiveness, then God would hear them and restore them to the land of their fathers. The devil did not want this consecrated Jew praying three times a day upon his knees in the direction of Jerusalem, and this was his way of preventing Israel's return to the land.

Notice in the scripture that Daniel did not know about the decree until after the king had signed it, and then it was too late to do anything about it. However, he did not allow the decree to interfere with his prayer life, or the presenting of petitions for his people before the Lord. The window in his apartment that was in the southwest corner was always left open, because this was the window that faced in the direction of Jerusalem, and as always, the first day after the decree was signed he knelt down three times before the window and prayed.

Daniel was Darius' right-hand man and probably the only man in all the kingdom in whom he could place complete confidence and trust. The king realized he had been tricked and blamed himself for being so stupid, and he thought all day until the sun went down on how he could find a loophole in the law whereby he could save his prime minister.

We continue and read Daniel 6:14-15: *"Then the king, when he heard these words, was sore displeased with himself, and set his heart on Daniel to deliver him: and he laboured till the going down of the sun to deliver him. Then these men assembled unto the king, and said unto the king, Know, O king, that the law of the Medes and Persians is, that no decree nor statute which the king establisheth may be changed."*

Most ancient laws stipulated execution of sentence within a matter of hours, usually the same day. Daniel had to be thrown into a den of angry, hungry lions. As the sun went down, the conspirators appeared before the king to again remind him that it was time for the sentence against Daniel to be carried out.

We continue and read Daniel 6:16-17: *"Then the king commanded, and they brought Daniel, and cast him into the den of lions. Now the king spake and said unto Daniel, Thy God whom thou servest continually, he will deliver thee. And a stone was brought, and laid upon the mouth of the den; and the king sealed it with his own signet, and with the signet of his lords; that the purpose might not be changed concerning Daniel."*

In verse sixteen we see revealed that Daniel had a wonderful testimony before this heathen king, because Darius admired Daniel for serving his God continually. Although Daniel's God was not the god of Darius, the king respected a faith that commanded such dedication.

The king, being unable to find a way out of the maddening legal situation, finally ordered Daniel to be brought before him for the carrying out of the sentence for breaking the king's law.

The conspirators were gathered around to make sure that Daniel really did go into the lion's den, and after the door was shut, they put two wax seals on it. One seal was signed by themselves, and one by the king. When they would come to the lions' den in the morning, they wanted to be sure the door had not been opened during the night.

We continue and read Daniel 6:18-20: *"Then the king went to his palace, and passed the night fasting: neither were instruments of musick brought before him: and his sleep went from him. Then the king arose very early in the morning, and went in haste unto the den of lions. And when he came to the den, he cried with a lamentable voice unto Daniel: and the king spake and said to Daniel, O Daniel, servant of the living God, is thy God, whom thou servest continually, able to deliver thee from the lions?"*

The king had told Daniel that the God who the prophet served would protect him through the night, but he didn't have much faith. He spent the night pacing the floor, and as soon as it was daylight, he hurried out of the palace to the lion pit.

We continue and read Daniel 6:21-24: *"Then said Daniel unto the king, O king, live for ever. My God hath sent his angel, and hath shut the lions' mouths, that they have not hurt me: forasmuch as before him innocency was found in me; and also before thee, O king, have I done no hurt. Then was the king exceeding glad for him, and commanded that they should take Daniel up out of the den. So Daniel was taken up out of the den, and no manner of hurt was found upon him, because he believed in his God. And the king commanded, and they brought those men which had accused Daniel, and they cast them into the den of lions, them, their children, and their wives; and the lions had the mastery of them, and brake all their bones in pieces or ever they came at the bottom of the den."*

The king had been up all night pacing the floor, sick with worry, half hoping and half doubting. With bloodshot eyes, ruffled hair, and unkempt clothing, he rushed to the pit and with a pitiful voice, he cried for Daniel. But Daniel had been sleeping peacefully all night long. Although he had been in the lions' den, Daniel was in much better shape than the king. And so the prophet raised himself up from among the lions, and with the wave of his hand, he saluted Darius with the traditional greeting: "O king, live for ever."

The scripture informs us that God sent His angel to shut the lions' mouths. As to which angel this was, we are not told. Another meaning for angel is messenger, and in a sense, Jesus Christ was God's angel, or messenger to the world. The angel could have been Michael. Michael is God's guardian angel over Israel (Rev. 12:7-9), and it was imperative that Daniel live to set the stage for Israel's return to the land after the Babylonian captivity.

In the experience of Daniel in the lions' den, we

again see how those things which happened to him and his three Hebrew companions look forward in type to the tribulation period. The rock which struck the feet of the image represents the Lord Jesus Christ at His second coming to put down all rule and authority; the madness which seized Nebuchadnezzar is symbolic of the madness of the Gentiles in their opposition to God's will to seat His Anointed as King of kings upon the holy hill of Zion; the deliverance of the three Hebrew children from the fiery furnace is a type of the way in which God will protect the 144,000 witnesses of Israel through the fiery judgment of the tribulation (Rev. 14:1-4); the drunken feast of Belshazzar on the night that Babylon fell is representative of the mass immorality and apostasy that grips the Gentile nations in the tribulation night; the deliverance of Daniel from the lions' den depicts the way in which God will protect Israel from the devil who devours like a roaring lion (1 Pet. 5:8).

As Daniel climbed the stairs from the lions' den, probably rubbing the sleep out of his eyes, he informed the king that God saved him for two reasons. The first reason was that he was innocent of hurting the king or challenging his authority. But let us not read into Daniel 6:22 something that isn't there. Daniel did not plead innocent of breaking the law, for indeed what he did was in violation of the law of the land. He was guilty of violating the law of the Medes and Persians. Regardless of how inane or unjustifiable this law was, Daniel must pay the penalty. He was tried, convicted, and his sentence was carried out. This was all according to the will of God. God would not intervene until the law had been satisfied (Rom. 13:1-4).

Darius himself admitted that Daniel had violated a bad law, but nevertheless, this did not lessen to any degree the king's responsibility to enforce the law nor Daniel's obligation to the state to suffer the penalty which the law demanded. Human government stands or falls solely upon the basis of law enforcement. If people lose the will to enforce the law, then lawlessness and chaos prevails.

In Daniel's case, the letter of the law was fulfilled. Daniel was cast into the lions' den according to the penalty of the law. The law did not demand that the lions eat him. God saved Daniel because he was found innocent of any intent to harm Darius or challenge his authority.

After Daniel was brought up safely from the lions' den, King Darius was exceedingly glad, and he commanded that the conspirators and all their families be brought forth and cast into the lion's den. And when they were placed in the pit, the lions were on them the minute they were pushed through the gate, and they were all dead even before any reached the bottom of the stairs. Some may protest that this was a cruel and inhuman thing to do and God should have stopped the slaughter. But God had nothing to do with the execution of Daniel's enemies. They had condemned themselves. These conspirators could have repented of their sins and believed in God, but they chose rather to reject the truth which God had set before them in the person of His prophet Daniel.

We continue and read the last four verses of the sixth chapter: *"Then king Darius wrote unto all people, nations, and languages, that dwell in all the earth; Peace be multiplied unto you. I make a decree, that in every dominion of my kingdom men tremble and fear before the God of Daniel: for he is the living God, and stedfast for ever, and his kingdom that which shall not be destroyed, and his dominion shall be even unto the end. He delivereth and rescueth, and he worketh signs and wonders in heaven and in earth, who hath delivered Daniel from the power of the lions. So this Daniel prospered in the reign of Darius, and in the reign of Cyrus the Persian"* (Dan. 6:25-28).

Those who conspired to cause the death of an innocent man were, in the final analysis, caught in their own trap. Josephus explains that the reason the king cast them all in with the lions was that they failed to give God the glory. They accused the king of feeding the lions so much they were not hungry. Therefore, the king told them that if the lions were full of food, then let them prove it by going into the den themselves. Josephus also relates that because Daniel was so highly regarded, he built a tower at Ecbatana in Media, and in 80 A.D., the historian said that it was just as beautiful as the day it was built. It was used by the Medes and Persians to entomb the dead members of the royal family.

Whether Darius was saved through the testimony of Daniel is a matter of opinion. He certainly confessed the God of Daniel as the living God, and the Ruler of all people and nations, and the One who delivers those who believe in Him from the powers of evil. It would appear that this profession of faith by Darius would indicate that he was saved.

Chapter Seven

"In the first year of Belshazzar king of Babylon Daniel had a dream and visions of his head upon his bed: then he wrote the dream, and told the sum of the matters" (Dan. 7:1).

We buried Belshazzar at the conclusion of chapter five, but at the beginning of chapter seven we find him very much alive. Some may well wonder whether or not this Babylonian king has come back from the dead in the interim of chapter six. However, by considering the entire context of the statement concerning Belshazzar, it is easily discernable that the first six chapters of Daniel constitute a historical account of world empires, and the last six chapters an apocalyptical view of things to come. In the first six chapters Daniel interpreted two dreams for Nebuchadnezzar and the handwriting on the wall for Belshazzar. Also included in the first six chapters are the accounts of the three Hebrews in the fiery furnace and Daniel in the lions' den. Both stories have an important end-time application. The historical part of Daniel has been fully vindicated by history. Josephus admitted in the year 80 A.D. that enough of Daniel had been fulfilled in his day to merit God's stamp of approval upon it as an inspired and divine book of prophecy. Quoting Josephus:

". . . It is fit to give an account of what this man did, which is most admirable to hear, for he was so happy as to have strange revelations made to him, and those as to one of the greatest of the prophets, insomuch, that while he was alive he had the esteem and applause both of the kings and of the multitude; and now he is dead, he retains a remembrance that will never fail, for the several books that he wrote and left behind him are still read by us till this time; and from them we believe that Daniel conversed with God; for he did not only prophesy of future events, as did other prophets, but he also determined the time of their accomplishment. And while prophets used to foretell misfortunes, and on that account were disagreeable both to the kings and to the multitude, Daniel was to them a prophet of good things, and this to such a degree, that by the agreeable nature of his predictions, he procured the good will of all men; and by the accomplishment of them, he procured the belief of their truth."

Josephus gave Daniel the credit for being unusually favored of God. So unusual and unique were the prophecies he made that he swayed even the leaders of nations to believe in the truth of God — so said the historian. If the book of Daniel could lead men, even heathen rulers, to believe in God two thousand years ago, how much more should we use this book to persuade men to repent and turn to God today. The very culmination of the prophetic importance of this book, the institution of the King of Heaven and earth, is rising up before our very eyes.

Josephus said that Daniel wrote several books. Several would usually mean four or five, and it would appear that Daniel was originally divided into four divisions, with one division coming at the end of chapter six. Books in Daniel's day were written on scrolls, and often two or three scrolls would comprise an entire book. Daniel separated his apocalyptic experiences from back in time at the beginning of chapter seven to pick up the account of those prophecies which were revealed directly to him by vision or by angels.

Belshazzar ruled for three years, and as we have pointed out, he ruled in a subservient position to Nabonidus as the second ruler of the kingdom. In the first year of Belshazzar's reign Daniel received a vision from God. At this particular time, Daniel had fallen from favor in the court, but God was not through with him. This was in the year 541 B.C., three years before the fall of Babylon. Inasmuch as Belshazzar, or the date, does not figure into the revelation itself, it can be surmised that Daniel gave the time he received the revelation in order to show us that from chapter six, the book does not necessarily continue in chronological order. We read more about this dream Daniel had in the next two verses: *"Daniel spake and said, I saw in my vision by night, and, behold, the four winds of the heaven strove upon the great sea. And four great beasts came up from the sea, diverse one from another"* (Dan. 7:2-3).

The prophet was very explicit in what he saw, and the fact that he emphasized that he witnessed these things with his own eyes points out that this vision was real. Some seem to believe that just because the Scriptures say this happened in a vision, we can take it with a grain of salt. But a vision is a revelation from Heaven. A person's eyes may play tricks on him, but something that is seen in a Heavensent vision is beyond human error. Nine times in chapter seven Daniel says: "I saw," "I beheld," or "I was beholding."

As we have noted in the Revelation, and in some of the books of prophecy in the Old Testament, the language is symbolic. This is nearly always the case in a direct revelation from Heaven. In these two verses, we find four symbolic expressions: by night, the four winds of Heaven, the great sea, and four great beasts.

The expression "by night" gives the time of day in which Daniel received the revelation. There is a definite reason why Daniel recorded that this vision from Heaven was given to him during the night. The "day of God's wrath," the seven-year period at the end of the age in which national rebellions against the sovereignty of God will be dealt with, is consistently referred to in the prophecies as "the night," or a time of darkness. We read of the day of the Lord's wrath in Joel 2:2: *"A day of darkness and of gloominess, a day of clouds and of thick darkness, as the morning spread* upon the mountains. . . ." We also read in 1 Thessalonians 5:2: *"For yourselves know perfectly that the day of the Lord so cometh as a thief in the night."*

Therefore this vision that Daniel received in the night signified that it concerned the tribulation period at the end of this present age. We read in the interpretation of the vision, the Lord will come with the clouds of Heaven and dispel the night with the brightness of His glorious presence.

The second symbolic expression is "the four winds of Heaven." There is a difference of opinion among fundamental prophetic scholars as to what the four winds of Heaven refer. Some believe that the four winds refer to the divine will of God that flows throughout the universe. If this is the correct interpretation, then the entire course of events represented in the vision is according to the providential will of the Creator. Others believe that the four winds refer to the storms of rebellion which Satan uses to disrupt the order that God established in creation. We know that there are nuclear winds that flow through outer space, but it seems readily apparent that the winds Daniel mentioned are forces which stir up nations to defy the God of Heaven. The fact that they blow from all points on the compass indicates their universality. In Revelation 7:1 we are informed that before the judgments of the tribulation begin, God will send four angels to hold back the four winds of the earth. The "four winds of the earth" are literal winds that blow back and forth across the earth, the stirring of the atmosphere. It is evident that there will be a nuclear war during the tribulation, and God will hold back the winds for a little while to prevent the spread of atomic fallout, until the 144,000 Jewish evangelists out of all nations are sealed by the Lord's divine protection. But the four winds of Heaven are not to be confused with the four winds of the earth.

It is evident from Ephesians 6:12 and many other scriptures that Satan has his powers and rulers of darkness in heavenly places to foment unbelief and rebellion throughout the universe, and these agents of darkness continually attack the world. Although what happens to the world will be by permission of the providence of God, the winds themselves would seem to be of a satanic origin. Upon the earth we have high pressure areas that bring fair weather, and low pressure areas which bring with them violent storms. It is the continual struggle between high pressure and low pressure that create the winds, and there is a similar struggle going on in the heavens — the high forces of God against the low powers of evil.

The third symbolic expression mentioned by Daniel in these two verses is "the great sea." The human mass is spoken of symbolically throughout the Bible as the restless sea. Nations considered individually are called seas. We read in Revelation 17:15: "*. . . The waters which thou sawest . . . are peoples, and multitudes, and nations, and tongues.*" We read of an end-time description of nations in Isaiah 17:12: "*Woe to the multitude of many people, which make a* *noise like the noise of the seas; and to the rushing of nations, that make a rushing like the rushing of mighty waters!"* There are at least eight places in the Old Testament where the Mediterranean Sea is called "the great sea." For example, we read in Joshua 15:12: *"And the west border* [of Israel] *was to the great sea. . . ."* Therefore, it would seem that the "great sea" of Daniel 7:2 refers to the nations surrounding the Mediterranean area.

The fourth expression is "four great beasts." God looks upon nations, and leaders of nations who are completely humanistic and who have completely divorced themselves from any recognition of the sovereignty of God in the affairs of men and nations as beasts, as beastlike in thought and deed. When Nebuchadnezzar claimed all the honor and glory to himself and departed from God's will in the affairs of government, God made him to look and act as he really was — a dumb ox. We read in Revelation chapter thirteen that the Antichrist, the last world ruler, is called a beast.

In these four introductory expressions to Daniel's vision, we can determine that four great world powers will be stirred up by the powers of Satan to rise up in the Mediterranean area.

Daniel saw the great sea, and the great sea is identified in Scripture as the Mediterranean Sea. As Daniel beheld the sea, the four winds of Heaven began to blow against it — first from one direction and then another. The wind blew from the west, it blew from the east, it blew from the north, and it blew from the south, and the sea became a swirling, churning mass of waves and turbulent waters. As he watched the stormy sea, beasts began to come up out of the sea — four in number. The storm awakened these dormant monsters, and they came forth to prowl upon the earth. All four beasts were predators — flesh-eating animals.

Let us continue and read Daniel 7:4-8: *"The first was like a lion, and had eagle's wings: I beheld till the wings thereof were plucked, and it was lifted up from the earth, and made stand upon the feet as a man, and a man's heart was given to it. And behold another beast, a second, like to a bear, and it raised up itself on one side, and it had three ribs in the mouth of it between the teeth of it: and they said thus unto it, Arise, devour much flesh. After this I beheld, and lo another, like a leopard, which had upon the back of it four wings of a fowl; the beast had also four heads; and dominion was given to it. After this I saw in the night visions, and behold a fourth beast, dreadful and terrible, and strong exceedingly; and it had great iron teeth: it devoured and brake in pieces, and stamped the residue with the feet of it: and it was diverse from all the beasts that were before it; and it had ten horns. I considered the horns, and, behold, there came up among them another little horn, before whom there were three of the first horns plucked up by the roots: and, behold, in this horn were eyes like the eyes of man, and a mouth speaking great things."*

The generally accepted interpretation of Daniel's vision concerning the four beasts corresponds to the four divisions of the image which Nebuchadnezzar saw in a dream. The beast like a lion with eagle's wings is Babylon; the bear with three ribs in his mouth is Medo-Persia; the beast like a leopard with four wings of a fowl is Greece; and the last beast, which was too dreadful and terrible for Daniel to describe, is Rome.

The reason Bible scholars have given this interpretation to this vision in Daniel chapter seven is that the lion is the king of the beasts, and therefore the lion represented Babylon. The plucking off of the eagle's wings related to Nebuchadnezzar's downfall and his period of insanity. Thereafter, he was lifted from his beastlike existence and restored to his kingdom. The reason the bear is identified with the Medo-Persian Empire is because it is a huge lumbering beast, and the Medo-Persian military victories were due to its commitment to huge forces to battle whereby enemies were overcome by the superiority of numbers. The three ribs in the bear's mouth represent the triple alliance of Babylon, Egypt, and Lydia against Medo-Persia. After the bear comes the leopard. According to the traditional explanation, this beast is descriptive of the Grecian Empire. Just as the leopard is smaller and more swift in motion than the other beasts mentioned, Alexander overcame opposing armies with tactical superiority and maneuverability, even though he had a smaller military force. The terrible beast with iron teeth represents the Roman Empire, with the ten horns referring to the Revived Roman Empire and the little horn representative of Antichrist.

There are many prophecies which have an initial, or representative fulfillment, but the literal or ultimate fulfillment is not accomplished until a later date. Many Catholic and Protestant theologians have contended that all the prophecies of Jesus Christ in the Olivet Discourse were fulfilled at the destruction of Jerusalem and the temple by Titus in 70 A.D.; however, an impartial judgment of the facts indicates that the prophecies of Jesus in Matthew chapter twenty-four were fulfilled only in type in 70 A.D. This mini-interpretation of prophecy has given rise to A-millennialism and post-millennialism.

The Abomination of Desolation spoken of by Daniel has been interpreted to have been fulfilled when Antiochus offered a sow upon the altar in the temple. But according to Jesus Christ, it will not be fulfilled literally until the Antichrist sits in the temple during the tribulation.

It has been our observation that the prophecies which God gave to the prophets of Israel had one common denominator: the kingdom promise. This was the one thing that concerned all the prophets: When will the Messiah come to Israel and fulfill the covenants? When will the Christ come and make Israel the head of God's kingdom of nations upon earth? While many of these prophecies had an initial fulfillment, or a covenant confirmation, the second application is of far greater importance, the consummation of these prophecies pertain literally to the bringing in of the kingdom at the second advent of Christ.

As declared by Josephus, Daniel was the greatest of the Old Testament prophets because he was explicit in his prophetic applications. He mentioned kingdoms by name and even gave the time in which his prophecies would be fulfilled. When Daniel interpreted Nebuchadnezzar's dream about the image, he pointed to the king and declared: *"Thou art the head of gold!"* The rest of the image fell into their proper places with the fall and rise of subsequent empires. When the prophet interpreted Nebuchadnezzar's dream about the tree, he again pointed to the monarch and said: *"It is thou, O king!"* Again, when he was called to interpret the handwriting on the wall, he boldly told Belshazzar: *"Thou art weighed in the balance, and art found wanting. . . . Thy kingdom is given to the Medes and Persians."* The prophet was again explicit in the interpretation of the vision about the ram and the goat. He boldly stated that Greece would be victorious over Medo-Persia, and this was two hundred years before the rise of the Grecian Empire. Josephus gives all these prophecies as a witness to Daniel's greatness in the service of God; however, the historian does not even make mention of the vision of the four beasts. The reason for the omission is apparent. No one to that time, about 80 A.D., had connected the lion with eagle's wings as Babylon, the bear with three ribs in its mouth as Medo-Persia, or the leopard as Greece. If the lion did indeed represent Babylon, why did not Daniel declare it? It is apparent from the ending of chapter seven that Daniel didn't know who these beasts represented, and it is apparent from Josephus that no one had connected them to nations or empires existing in his time. Daniel knew only one thing about the rise of the four beasts, and that was, when the last beast was standing upon the great sea, the Lord would come to bring in His kingdom. Therefore, it is difficult to understand how anyone could be so dogmatic as to say that the lion has to be ancient Babylon, the bear has to be Medo-Persia, and the leopard has to be Greece. The forces of Satan deceiving the nations, and preparing them to be drawn into the Middle East at the battle of Armageddon; the waves and the seas roaring; wars and rumors of wars; the major world powers' interest in the Mediterranean — all these things would place the setting entirely in the last generation. In fact, never in the history of the world until now, have these four beasts been identifiable according to national emblems. However, all four beasts are very much in evidence today and all four are very much concerned about the Mediterranean Sea.

With the signing of the Balfour Declaration recognizing Palestine as the rightful home of the Jews, the hands of God's prophetic clock began to move. Prophetic history of the Middle East from that time to the second coming of Christ is revealed in the seventh chapter of Daniel. In Daniel 7:4 we notice that the first predatory beast is a lion with eagle's wings, and Daniel saw this lion coming up out of the Mediterranean Sea. After World War I, England dictated policy in the Middle East. The national symbol of England is the lion. We read in *Webster's Dictionary*: "**Lion***: a large, powerful mammal of the animal family, found in Africa and southwest Asia. . . . It is also the symbol of Great Britain.*" From 1918 to 1948, the Mediterranean Sea was an English sea. English ships sailed past Gibraltar, then on to the Suez Canal, and then on down to the Indian Ocean, and fluttering from the highest mast on each ship was the bold and fearless lion of Great Britain.

Next we notice that the lion Daniel saw had on its back eagle's wings, and as it walked upon the Mediterranean Sea, the wings were plucked off. We read again from *Webster's Dictionary*: "**Eagle***: any of a number of large, strong, flesh-eating birds of prey belonging to the falcon family. . . . The national emblem of the United States.*" Wings, when spoken of symbolically in the Scriptures, indicate protection. Over and over in the Old Testament we read of God's protective wings over Israel. Jesus declared in Matthew 23:37 that He would have gathered Jerusalem like a mother hen protects her chicks under her wings, but they would not. The United States, since World War I, has been England's protective wings. This nation had to come to England's aid in World War I and again in World War II, but England and the United States have drifted apart and England has declined as a world colonial power. We notice in Daniel's account in the vision, that as the eagle-wings are plucked off, the lion no longer is a predatory beast, but stands up and becomes a man. No longer is the lion the hunter, but rather as a man he becomes the hunted and must fear other predators. Since World War II, England has lost its dominion. Today England is a relatively weak nation. However, with the withdrawal of England from the Mediterranean after World War II, the eagle's wings that were plucked off, the United States, controlled the great sea. Thus, for twenty years the Mediterranean was an American sea and the United States dictated policy in the Middle East. We remember President Eisenhower intervening to make Israel and England return the Suez Canal to Nasser, and then again when he landed Marines in Lebanon. But the area of American control over the Mediterranean and the surrounding territory began slipping in 1968 with the appearance of a superior Russian armada upon the scene.

The four beasts seen by Daniel are flesh-eating animals — predators. Empires act like beasts because there is only one way a nation becomes an empire: by devouring much flesh; by conquering other nations and then digesting them into a colonial system. As the eagle's wings are plucked off of the lion, it stands on its feet like a man and a man's heart was given to it (Dan. 7:4). The old saying that the sun never sets on the British Empire is no longer true. England has been divesting itself of its colonial system since World War II, and not only is England not beastlike any longer, the English have lost all heart for either restoring or even maintaining what is left of the British Empire.

Let us reconsider the second beast that is seen by Daniel coming upon the Mediterranean Sea. *"And behold another beast, a second, like to a bear, and it raised up itself on one side, and it had three ribs in the mouth of it between the teeth of it: and they said thus unto it, Arise, devour much flesh"* (Dan. 7:5).

The United States is identified by the eagle, and it was no coincidence that the eagle was chosen to be our national emblem. Although the eagle is not a beast, it is a predatory bird. As a nation, the United States has never tried to conquer and devour other people in order to build an empire, but neither have we failed in courage to fight where our own needs and self-interest have been involved. After the departure of the lion from the Mediterranean, the eagle's wings lingered for twenty years. But the failure of the United States to fulfill contractual commitments to Israel in the Six-Day War of June 1967 marked the decline of U.S. naval power in the Mediterranean and the total collapse of our political influence in the Middle East outside the borders of Israel. On God's prophetic clock, it was time for the bear to take its bath in the great sea.

What emblem, besides the hammer and sickle, is Russia known by? By the sign of the bear, of course. One can go anywhere in the world and find that

Russia is always identified in the press by the cartoon drawing of a giant lumbering bear. Nations have flags to identify them according to their political or racial structure, but they also adopt another symbol which identifies them according to national disposition. If you were to go to the zoo in your area and ask the keepers what animal they consider to be the most dangerous, they would likely say the bear. Most zookeepers say the bears are even more dangerous than the lions and tigers because not only can they claw and bite, but they can reach out and kill a person with a powerful stroke of one of the front legs. They are so huge and strong that a man has little chance of escape once he comes in contact with a wild or angry bear. Certainly, the bear is a fitting emblem of the national nature of Russia, because Russia is the most dangerous of all the predatory nations in modern times. It is big and cumbersome, yet tenacious and fierce.

With this in mind, let us read again Daniel 7:5: *"And behold another beast, a second, like to a bear, and it raised up itself on one side, and it had three ribs in the mouth of it between the teeth of it: and they said thus unto it, Arise, devour much flesh."* With the text of this verse we see a hungry bear with three bony ribs in its mouth. As it rises up on one side, the ribs, in a most precarious predicament themselves, speak to the bear and say: "Arise, devour much flesh." The traditional interpretation that the three ribs represent the ancient nations of Babylonia, Egypt, and Lydia does not satisfy the meaning. Why would Babylonia, Egypt, and Lydia entreat Medo-Persia to embark on aggression? They wouldn't because Medo-Persia was the enemy. What we actually have represented is a dangerous accommodation arrangement like the one existing between Russia and the Arab world. The Arabs are indeed in a most precarious position — trying to use the power of the bear by whetting its appetite, yet without being chewed up and swallowed by the beast. Russia has invested billions in the Middle East, but has yet to reap much harvest. The Arabs cannot keep Russia pacified forever, because the bear is out for bigger game — the Middle East oil fields, the Suez Canal, the riches of the Dead Sea, and the new cities, farms, and factories in Israel. Today the Russian bear is rising up one side toward the Mediterranean, as indicated in Daniel 7:5.

We definitely believe the three ribs in the bear's mouth represent three nations. It seems apparent that three nations in the Middle East from the Arab bloc will fall upon Russia to fulfill its military commitments and attack Israel. This is evident in their calling on the bear to rise and devour much flesh. The result of Russia's invasion of Israel is clearly prophesied in Ezekiel: *"And I will call for a sword against him throughout all my mountains, saith the Lord God: every man's sword shall be against his brother. And I will plead against him with pestilence and with blood: and I will rain upon him, and upon his bands, and upon the many people that are with him, an*

*overflowing rain, and great hailstones, fire, and brim-
stone. . . . Thou shalt fall upon the mountains of Israel,
thou, and all thy bands. . . .* " (Ezek. 38:21-22; 39:4).

We also read what happens to the great army
from the north that invades Israel in the last days in
Joel 2:20: ". . . *I will remove far off from you the
northern army, and will drive him into a land barren
and desolate, with his face toward the east sea, and his
hinder part toward the utmost sea, and his stink shall
come up, and his ill savour shall come up, because he
hath done great things.*"

The Russian army will be driven back all the way
to Siberia, because Siberia lies between the Pacific
Ocean (the east sea) and the Arctic Ocean (the utmost
sea). But after the bear is chased from the
Mediterranean Sea back to its northern lair licking its
wounds, another predator enters the great sea. This
beast will be a leopard.

Russia will not control the Mediterranean forever.
In fact, we fully expect Russia's domination of the
Mediterranean and the Middle East to be a relatively
short period. However, we know from Ezekiel chapters
thirty-eight and thirty-nine that God will intervene
and the armies of Russia that are sent against Israel
will suffer a terrible defeat, and the communist hold
on the Mediterranean area will be broken. What
power bloc will control the Mediterranean after the
defeat of Russia?

As we have stated before, we believe the attempt
by Russia to invade Israel will come soon after the

tribulation begins. The prophecies are clear in that the kingdom of Antichrist will control the Middle East for the last three and a half years of the tribulation, but from the time Russia is thrown out of this part of the world until the middle of the tribulation, an interim power must be the dominating influence. The beast that appears on the scene after the defeat of Russia is described in Daniel 7:6: *"After this I beheld, and lo another, like a leopard, which had upon the back of it four wings of a fowl; the beast had also four heads; and dominion was given to it."*

After the bear is chased from the Mediterranean, the four-headed leopard with four wings on its back appears. We cannot tell a great deal about this particular beast, because it has not made its appearance yet, and it cannot appear until after the battle of Ezekiel chapters thirty-eight and thirty-nine. Leopards are not native to Palestine; however, from the Song of Solomon 4:8, it is evident that there were some of these animals in the mountains to the south of Israel. The leopard is a ferocious beast and relatively small in comparison to a bear or lion. According to Jeremiah 5:6 and Hosea 13:7, we know they stalk their prey. While the nature of a lion is of a kingly bearing, protective toward its family, methodical in its hunting habits, and reticent to attack either man or other wild beast except when its domain is threatened, the characteristics of the third Mediterranean power is strikingly different from either the lion or the bear. The leopard is a cunning animal with seemingly no self-protective instincts. It is one of the few animals in the world that will attack a man without provocation. The native habitat of the leopard is the southern region of Asia and all of Africa with the exception of the desert areas. It is especially native to central Africa.

While the lion is the national emblem of England, the bear of Russia, the eagle of the United States, no nation of international prominence claims the leopard as its representative symbol. However, the leopard has been the symbol of rising black nationalism in Africa. Black nationalistic terrorist groups in Africa of the past three decades have adopted the leopard as their standard. The Mau Mau terrorists and other similar African organizations have worn leopard skins and fashioned weapons out of leopard claws tied or nailed to clubs and boards.

The nature and characteristics of this third beast are indicative of the African bloc of nations, or an Afro-Asian alliance. The Asian nations would certainly be those of Southwest Asia. The African bloc in the United Nations has been demanding a greater voice in Middle Eastern affairs. Some of these African spokesmen have invited both the United States and Russia to get out of the Middle East. Today, there is a loose-knit African alliance that is associated with the Common Market. These African nations are former French, Belgium, Netherland, and German colonies. These nations are Tunisia, Morocco, Central African Republic, Gabon, Congo, Republic of the Congo, Uganda, Tanzania, Kenya, Somalia, and five other smaller nations. These nations are associate members of the Common Market. These are also nations that are native to the leopard.

We read in Daniel 7:6 of the leopard kingdom that "dominion was given to it." This is said of none of the other three beasts. Now, why would Daniel say this of only the leopard empire? If the leopard applied to Greece, then we would indeed have a difficult time explaining the meaning because Alexander was a classic of all the conquerors who either preceded or succeeded him. He overcame and took the Middle East just like Nebuchadnezzar, Cyrus, or the caesars — by raw military power. When England took possession of the Mediterranean, they simply moved their fleet in and said: "We're it. Who is strong enough to put us out?" Likewise, the United States and now Russia.

The fact that dominion will be given to the leopard kingdom would indicate that the next Mediterranean power that will control the Middle East will receive its authority from an outside source. The leopard kingdom will not have sufficient military power of itself to control the great sea, but it will receive an appointment and sufficient strength to enforce its will. This appointment may come from the United Nations or by direct agreement from several stronger nations. Of course, the African nations, membership-wise, constitute the strongest bloc in the United Nations.

Next, we notice that the four-headed leopard has

four wings on its back. In the traditional interpretation, the four heads refer to four provinces, or divisions, of the Grecian Empire, and the four wings are symbolic of rulers. Horns are representative of kings and sovereigns (Dan. 7:8; 8:7-9; Rev. 17:12). And neither are wings representative of speed. Wings are used symbolically in the Scriptures to indicate either godly protection or an outside protective power (Ps. 17:8: *". . . hide me under the shadow of thy wings"*; Jer. 49:22: *". . . he shall come up and fly as the eagle, and spread his wings over Bozrah . . ."*). The wings on the back of the leopard are nearly as strong as the wings on the lion. The lion has eagle's wings, but the leopard has the wings of a fowl. Again we see that the leopard empire will be weaker in strength than the other three beasts. We do not propose to know exactly what the four heads and four wings represent, and there is no way of knowing until it appears upon the world scene. The description of this coming puppet empire in the Middle East according to symbolism is as follows:

1. It will be composed of a group of African nations, and possibly some of the nations from Southwest Asia.
2. It will rule and exercise authority by permission from an outside source, and probably the United Nations, with a protective rule over it by four outside stronger powers.
3. It will be much weaker in military power than the other three empires.

4. It will come upon the scene after Russia invades Israel.
5. Its existence will be brief, and it will be replaced by the kingdom of Antichrist.

In the book of Revelation we read that the kings of the East will become vitally concerned about the Mediterranean area, and they will bring their armies across the Euphrates River.

The thing that is bringing all nations into the Middle East, as prophesied in the Bible for the latter days, is oil. Existing oil reserves in other areas of the world are already insufficient to feed the growing world of machines, and as time goes on, black gold will become more valuable than yellow gold. God's Word is sure — all nations will be brought together in the Middle East at the battle of Armageddon.

The duration of the leopard kingdom will be brief — existing only from the defeat of Russia until the appearance of Antichrist. We continue and read about the fourth beast: *"After this I saw in the night visions, and behold a fourth beast, dreadful and terrible, and strong exceedingly; and it had great iron teeth: it devoured and brake in pieces, and stamped the residue with the feet of it: and it was diverse from all the beasts that were before it; and it had ten horns"* (Dan. 7:7).

In all confidence we can say that this dreadful and terribly beastly monstrosity represents the kingdom of Antichrist. Daniel saw this beast devouring the flesh of all people; he saw it breaking the nations into pieces; and what it could not devour and break, it utterly stomped underneath its feet into the earth. There appears to be no escape from this beast for anyone on the earth. We read of the Antichrist in Revelation 13:7: *"And it was given unto him to make war with the saints, and to overcome them: and power was given him over all kindreds, and tongues, and nations."*

In Daniel's interpretation of the fourth beast we read in Daniel 7:23-24: *"Thus he said, The fourth beast shall be the fourth kingdom upon earth, which shall be diverse from all kingdoms, and shall devour the whole earth, and shall tread it down, and break it in pieces. And the ten horns out of this kingdom are ten kings that shall arise: and another shall rise after them; and he shall be diverse from the first, and he shall subdue three kings."*

The devil sends three beasts into the Middle East to prevent the refounding of Israel as a nation whereby Christ will return and rule on David's throne, but the first three beasts are not successful in their mission. And so the devil blows again on the great sea and the fourth beast appears, the most fearsome predator of all. We read of him in Revelation 12:12: *". . . Woe to the inhabiters of the earth and of the sea! for the devil is come down unto you, having great wrath, because he knoweth that he hath but a short time."*

No one on earth, even God's people, can stand

against this horrible creature. We read in Revelation
13:5, 7: *"And there was given unto him a mouth
speaking great things and blasphemies; and power
was given unto him to continue forty and two
months. . . . And it was given unto him to make war
with the saints, and to overcome them. . . ."*

We know according to Daniel 7:25 that the life of
this beast will be three and a half years. We read: *"And
he shall speak great words against the most High, and
shall wear out the saints of the most High, and think
to change times and laws: and they shall be given into
his hand until a time* [1 year] *and times* [2 years] *and
the dividing of time* [½ year]." A "time" on the
Hebrew calendar was from Pentecost to Pentecost, or
one year.

To prove beyond doubt that the fourth beast of
Daniel is the same beast that John saw in control of
the whole world during the last three and a half years
of the Great Tribulation, we read Revelation 13:1-5:
*"And I stood upon the sand of the sea, and saw a beast
rise up out of the sea, having seven heads and ten
horns, and upon his horns ten crowns, and upon his
heads the name of blasphemy. And the beast which I
saw was like unto a leopard, and his feet were as the
feet of a bear, and his mouth as the mouth of a lion:
and the dragon gave him his power, and his seat, and
great authority . . . and all the world wondered after
the beast. And they worshipped the dragon which
gave power unto the beast: and they worshipped the
beast, saying, Who is like unto the beast? who is able*

to make war with him? And there was given unto him a mouth speaking great things and blasphemies; and power was given unto him to continue forty and two months [3½ years]."

The reason we have gone to great detail in explaining that Daniel's fourth beast and the Antichrist (the beast which John described in Rev. 13), are the same is that there are important national identification characteristics afforded by John, and these are not given in Daniel. Daniel did not attempt to describe the animal characteristics of the fourth beast, but John does describe it. Daniel said that it was a "diverse beast" of all the three beasts which preceded it. This does not mean that it was an entirely different beast, but rather that it was a composite of the first three beasts. We read in the dictionary that one meaning of "diverse" is varied, or diversified. We read much today about businesses becoming diversified, that is, expanding their enterprises to include many commodities or products. Thus, it is proven again that Daniel's fourth beast and the beast kingdom of the Antichrist are the same, because the diversification is manifested in the three-part beast that John saw.

Having established this truth beyond point of controversy, we can readily determine that the kingdom of Antichrist will include the nations of Africa, the Arab nations, England, and Russia. We can determine this from the fact that the beast has the feet of a bear, the mouth of a lion, and a middle section like a leopard.

We have left out three great powers that are in evidence in the world at this time. These are: the United States, the Common Market nations of Europe, and the nations of the Far East. But before we consider the relationship of these three world powers to the kingdom of Antichrist, let us read Daniel 11:42-43: *"He shall stretch forth his hand also upon the countries: and the land of Egypt shall not escape. But he shall have power over the treasures of gold and of silver, and over all the precious things of Egypt: and the Libyans and the Ethiopians shall be at his steps."*

This scripture clearly indicates that the kingdom of Antichrist will include the African nations and the Arab nations. Let us continue and read Daniel 11:44-45: *"But tidings out of the east and out of the north shall trouble him: therefore he shall go forth with great fury to destroy, and utterly to make away many. And he shall plant the tabernacles of his palace between the seas in the glorious holy mountain; yet he shall come to his end, and none shall help him."*

We should remember that when God destroys the Russian army that will come against Israel, He will not destroy Russia itself. Although this disaster will greatly weaken Russia, the Soviets will still be able to make war. It is apparent that when Antichrist claims the Middle East as his territory and absorbs Egypt, Libya, and the African nations into his empire, the communist nations, which includes all the area to the north and east of Jerusalem, will rise up to challenge him. This will come at the midway point of the tribulation, and it will be at this time that Russia will be absorbed into his kingdom by right of conquest. We read of the entrance of the Far East nations into the tribulation arena of conflict in Revelation 16:12: *"And the sixth angel poured out his vial upon the great river Euphrates; and the water thereof was dried up, that the way of the kings of the east might be prepared."* The most powerful of the Eastern nations to head the kings of the East will be Red China.

We see nothing in the description of the fourth beasts that relates to an eagle. Inasmuch as the eagle-wings on the lion are clipped off before the arrival of Antichrist on the scene, it is clear that the United States will not be included in the kingdom of the last beast. Only the lion is taken into the last empire; the eagle is left behind.

We have fitted all the major powers into their respective positions to the Antichrist kingdom with the exception of the European Common Market nations. In order to bring these nations into view in our prophetic telescope, let us read more about the ten horns on the fourth beast in Daniel 7:8: *"I considered the horns, and, behold, there came up among them another little horn, before whom there were three of the first horns plucked up by the roots: and, behold, in this horn were eyes like the eyes of man, and a mouth speaking great things."*

We read more about the ten horns in Revelation 17:12-16: *"And the ten horns which thou sawest are ten kings, which have received no kingdom as yet; but receive power as kings one hour with the beast. These have one mind, and shall give their power and strength unto the beast. . . . And the ten horns . . . shall hate the whore* [mystery Babylon], *and shall make her desolate and naked. . . ."* The ten horns are ten nations which will form an alliance and bring to power the Antichrist, who is called the little horn by Daniel.

There has been much prophetic interest in both Europe and the Middle East during the past ten years in order to determine whether these ten nations that will become the center of the beast kingdom are Arab nations or Common Market nations. The Arab nations have been forming all kinds of alliances, and although there are actually thirteen of fourteen identifiable Arab states, the top ten have appeared at times to be somewhat in unison in their condemnation of Israel; at other times, they have disagreed violently. We ourselves seriously considered the possibility that the ten-nation federated kingdom of Antichrist would come up out of the Arab countries; that something would happen to bring ten of the Arab nations together. However, such a possibility appears rather remote as we carefully consider the facts.

First, we are told that these ten nations would give their power and strength unto the beast, and this power afforded by these ten nations would be sufficient to conquer the world. The Arab states, at least today, have little power and strength of their own. We must remember also that several of these Arab states will suffer military catastrophe when God destroys the armies of Russia and the Arab countries who invade Israel. We read also in Daniel 11:42-43 that Egypt will not escape out of his hand, and neither will Libya. If this was truly an Arab alliance, why would Egypt and Libya even try to escape? We are told in Daniel 11:41 that Edom, Moab, and Ammon, the present nation of Jordan, will be fortunate and escape. Again, if this is an Arab alliance, why would Jordan even desire to escape? If you consider those Arab nations that will be judged with Russia, and add to these those nations that will either escape or be overrun by Antichrist, there will not be enough Arab states left to form a united front composed of ten nations. Therefore, it is difficult to see how the ten-nation kingdom of Antichrist can be from the Middle East. And this leaves only one possibility — the Common Market nations of Europe, the last of the national power groups to consider.

There is a European federation existing at this very hour. It is not a vague and undefinable federation, such as the one suggested for the Arab nations. It is an alliance that is concrete with firm political, economic, and religious foundations.

It has long been conceded by historians that if Europe ever united, it could control the world. Just think of the power that could have been used on other nations had England, France, and Germany united in World War II. There would not have been an alliance of nations on earth that could have stopped them.

We continue and read Daniel 7:9-10: *"I beheld till the thrones were cast down, and the ancient of days did sit, whose garment was white as snow, and the hair of his head like the pure wool: his throne was like the fiery flame, and his wheels as burning fire. A fiery stream issued and came forth from before him: thousand thousands ministered unto him, and ten thousand times ten thousand stood before him: the judgment was set, and the books were opened."*

As Daniel watched this fourth terrible beast stand upon the earth with its ten horns pointing in all directions, the horns were broken off, signifying that the ten-nation federation which gave the beast its power and authority were destroyed. Now by whom were they destroyed? Certainly, not by earthly power because we read in Revelation 13 that no one on earth during the last half of the tribulation could make war with the beast. The ten-nation alliance is destroyed by the Lord Jesus Christ, also called the Alpha and Omega, the Beginning and the End, the One who is from everlasting to everlasting. In His incarnation in human flesh to redeem man from sin and reclaim the world from the devil, the Lord is called the Son of man. The scene which Daniel saw in Heaven as Jesus Christ prepares to return to slay the last beast is described in Revelation 1:13-14: *"And in the midst of the seven candlesticks one like unto the Son of man, clothed with a garment down to the foot, and girt about the paps with a golden girdle. His head and his hairs were white like wool, as white as snow; and his eyes were as a flame of fire."*

In the dispensations of God, He has dealt with man in innocence, conscience, human government, promise, law, and sovereign grace, but a day is coming soon when God will deal with man in judgment. The first order of judgment will be to judge Gentile power and authority which is centered in the fourth beast. The second order of judgment will be to judge the nations. The third order of judgment will be to judge those who have spurned God's offer of redemption by faith in His only begotten Son who gave Himself for the sins of the world.

The wheels of burning fire that Daniel saw are possibly celestial vehicles of the angels. When Christ comes to judge the kingdom of Antichrist, He will come with all His holy angels, and the scene is described for us in Isaiah 66:15-16: *"For, behold, the Lord will come with fire, and with his chariots like a whirlwind, to render his anger with fury, and his rebuke with flames of fire. For by fire and by his sword will the Lord plead with all flesh: and the slain of the Lord shall be many."*

Reading next Daniel 7:11: *"I beheld then because of the voice of the great words which the horn spake: I beheld even till the beast was slain, and his body destroyed, and given to the burning flame."* We read in Revelation 13:5 of the little horn on the beast: *"And there was given unto him a mouth speaking great things and blasphemies. . . ."* This ruler of the last beast empire will try to force every man, woman, and child to reject Christ as Savior and deny the existence of God, and then he will pass a universal law that everyone must fall down and worship him as God. The end of this anti-Christ, demon-possessed madman which Daniel saw is also described in Revelation 19:19-21: *"And I saw the beast, and the kings of the earth, and their armies, gathered together to make war against him that sat on the horse* [Christ], *and against his army. And the beast was taken, and with him the false prophet that wrought miracles before him, with which he deceived them that had received the mark of the beast, and them that worshipped his image. These both were cast alive into a lake of fire burning with brimstone. And the remnant were slain with the sword of him that sat upon the horse, which sword proceeded out of his mouth: and all the fowls were filled with their flesh."*

Thus, we see the demise of the last beast, the kingdom of Antichrist. The kings are killed and their armies destroyed, and then the little horn, the Antichrist, and his spiritual adviser, the false prophet, are taken by the angels and cast into the lake of fire.

We continue our study of the seventh chapter of Daniel by reading verse twelve: *"As concerning the rest of the beasts, they had their dominion taken away: yet their lives were prolonged for a season and time."*

This part of Daniel's vision extends beyond the destruction of the fourth beast kingdom. This relates to the future and not to the past. In other words, England, Russia, and the Afro-Asian alliance will be stripped of all their power and territories, but they will continue to exist as nations during the millennium. The song the British sing, "There will always be an England," may very well be true. The only empire that will be destroyed at the second coming of Christ will be the kingdom of Antichrist. The judgment of nations does not occur when Christ returns. It comes at the end of the millennium. We read in many places in the Old Testament that the riches of the Gentiles would come to Israel during the Kingdom Age, and the nation that will not serve Israel will be utterly cut off. *"When the Son of man shall come in his glory, and all the holy angels with him, then shall he sit upon the throne of his glory: And before him shall be gathered all nations: and he shall separate them one from another, as a shepherd divideth his sheep from the goats"* (Matt. 25:31-32).

We note that Daniel said these nations represented by the first three beasts would be preserved for a season and *time*, not a season and *a time*. There will be nations here on earth today that will pass into the new earth because we read in Revelation 21:24 that in the new earth the nations will walk in the light of the new Jerusalem.

We continue and read Daniel 7:13-14: *"I saw in the night visions, and, behold, one like the Son of man came with the clouds of heaven, and came to the Ancient of days, and they brought him near before him. And there was given him dominion, and glory, and a kingdom, that all people, nations, and languages, should serve him: his dominion is an everlasting dominion, which shall not pass away, and his kingdom that which shall not be destroyed."*

We read in Acts 1:9-11: *"And when he [Jesus] had spoken these things, while they beheld, he was taken up; and a cloud received him out of their sight. And while they looked stedfastly toward heaven as he went up, behold, two men stood by them in white apparel; Which also said, Ye men of Galilee, why stand ye gazing up into heaven? this same Jesus, which is taken up from you into heaven, shall so come in like manner as ye have seen him go into heaven."*

According to the vision which God gave Daniel, the Son of man, the Messiah of Israel, is coming from Heaven with the clouds of Heaven to establish a kingdom that will have dominion over all people, all nations, and all languages. We continue and read Daniel 7:15-18: *"I Daniel was grieved in my spirit in the midst of my body, and the visions of my head troubled me. I came near unto one of them that stood by, and asked him the truth of all this. So he told me, and made me know the interpretation of the things. These great beasts, which are four, are four kings, which shall arise out of the earth. But the saints of the most High shall take the kingdom, and possess the kingdom for ever, even for ever and ever."*

Though the vision was clear to Daniel in its revelation, he could not completely grasp its meaning, and so he asked for help in understanding it. The identity of the one who helped Daniel is not made known, but we assume it was an angel. We know that the Apostle John often consulted his angelic guide in the book of Revelation. And so the interpreter informed Daniel in verse seventeen that the four great beasts represent four kings, or kingdoms, that would arise in the future. The Word here is emphatic: *"These great beasts, which are four, are four kings, which shall arise. . . ."* In other words, the lion with eagle's wings could not have been Babylon. The interpreter informed Daniel in verse eighteen that in spite of these four beasts' empires, they would prowl the Mediterranean. The saints of the most High would possess the kingdom, the center of which will be Israel, the promised land, for ever and ever. The word "saints" appears in the Bible in both testaments, and it always refers to God's people. In the Old Testament it means Israel (Exo. 19:6; Matt. 27:52-53). Under grace in the Church Age, a saint is a Christian (1 Cor. 1:2; Eph. 1:1; Phil. 1:1). A saint is also a person who will be saved in the tribulation by refusing to take the mark of Antichrist because he believes in the true Christ (Rev. 13:7). But the saints referred to in Daniel 7:18 are Israel.

We continue and read Daniel 7:19-27: *"Then I would know the truth of the fourth beast, which was diverse from all the others, exceeding dreadful, whose teeth were of iron, and his nails of brass; which devoured, brake in pieces, and stamped the residue with his feet; And of the ten horns that were in his head, and of the other which came up, and before whom three fell; even of that horn that had eyes, and a mouth that spake very great things, whose look was more stout than his fellows. I beheld, and the same horn made war with the saints, and prevailed against them; Until the Ancient of days came, and judgment was given to the saints of the most High; and the time came that the saints possessed the kingdom. Thus he said, The fourth beast shall be the fourth kingdom upon earth, which shall be diverse from all kingdoms, and shall devour the whole earth, and shall tread it down, and break it in pieces. And the ten horns out of this kingdom are ten kings that shall arise: and another shall rise after them; and he shall be diverse from the first, and he shall subdue three kings. And he shall speak great words against the most High, and shall wear out the saints of the most High, and think to change times and laws: and they shall be given into his hand until a time and times and the dividing of time. But the judgment shall sit, and they shall take away his dominion, to consume and to destroy it unto the end. And the kingdom and dominion, and the greatness of the kingdom under the whole heaven, shall be given to the people of the saints of the most High, whose kingdom is an everlasting kingdom, and all dominions shall serve and obey him."*

We have dealt with much of the interpretation of Daniel's vision about the four beasts already; however, there are some additional facts here that warrant our attention. Daniel was particularly interested in the fourth beast because it was the ruler of this kingdom who would make war against Israel and prevail against them for a time. The fourth beast was also the strangest and most horrible of all the beasts, and it would be destroyed by the Messiah when He came to bring in His kingdom. So it would be natural that Daniel would want to know as much as possible about it.

In verse twenty we are informed that the look of the little horn will be more stout than the other ten horns. This indicates that the Antichrist will indeed be a strong personality and command world attention. It is also related that three of the ten horns will fall before him. There will evidently be a power struggle within the beast kingdom and three of the ten kings will be killed. This may be the same time that the Antichrist himself will be wounded unto death (Rev. 13:3).

In verses twenty and twenty-one we are informed that from the midway point of the tribulation until the return of Christ, the Antichrist and his kingdom will prevail against Israel. In other words, the Antichrist will be in control of Jerusalem and all who will not accept him as the Messiah will have to flee for their lives. This was prophesied by Jesus in Matthew 24:15-21: *"When ye therefore shall see the abomination of desolation, spoken of by Daniel the prophet, stand in the holy place, (whoso readeth, let him understand:) Then let them which be in Judaea flee into the mountains: Let him which is on the housetop not come down to take any thing out of his house: Neither let him which is in the field return back to take his clothes. And woe unto them that are with child, and to them that give suck in those days! But pray ye that your flight be not in the winter, neither on the sabbath day: For then shall be great tribulation, such as was not since the beginning of the world to this time, no, nor ever shall be."*

It is also indicated in Revelation 12:13-16 that God will have to intervene directly and protect the remnant of Israel in a place called "the wilderness" for three and a half years. Many believe this place to be in Petra, but it is also indicated that they may be scattered throughout the area that comprised ancient Edom and Moab. We read in Daniel 11:41 that Edom, Moab, and Ammon will escape out of the hands of Antichrist. How this will be accomplished, we have no way of knowing at this time. Neither do we know at this time which three nations out of the Revived Roman Empire will lose their leaders, but those in the tribulation who read the book of Daniel will recognize these prophetic fulfillments when they come to pass.

We are told in verse twenty-three that the kingdom of Antichrist will devour the whole earth and tread it down. No empire has ever accomplished this in history, but the Antichrist will become the first true ruler of the world. For the sake of Israel, the ancient lands of Edom, Moab, and Ammon will be able to throw off his yoke.

We continue and read Daniel 7:28: *"Hitherto is the end of the matter. As for me Daniel, my cogitations much troubled me, and my countenance changed in me: but I kept the matter in my heart."*

The revelation was completed. Nothing further was revealed and Daniel remained greatly troubled. No one could be informed about what was coming upon this world at the end of this present age without being troubled. As we behold our world even today, it is no wonder that Daniel was troubled. But the blessed hope as presented in this marvelous chapter of prophecy is the coming of the Son of man to save the world for both Jew and Gentile.

Chapter Eight

The eighth chapter of Daniel relates to another vision that Daniel had, and we begin by reading verse one: *"In the third year of the reign of king Belshazzar a vision appeared unto me, even unto me Daniel, after that which appeared unto me at the first."*

In the first year of the reign of Belshazzar, which would have been in the year 541 B.C., God gave Daniel the vision of the four beasts. In the third year of Belshazzar, God gave Daniel a second vision. We know the vision came before the fall of Babylon, because Belshazzar was killed the same night the city was conquered by the Medes and Persians. As long as the king is alive, dates are given in accordance with the years he has been on the throne. For example, until his death, the Japanese honored their emperor Hirohito by dating events according to his reign (e.g., the fiftieth year of Hirohito). When the emperor died, it became in the first year of the next heir to the throne. Thus, it was in the year 538 B.C. while Belshazzar was still on the throne that Daniel received this vision.

In chapter seven the last Gentile world empire, represented by the beast with ten horns, is killed by the conquering Christ returning to claim the world for Himself; thus, the times of the Gentiles end. From verse four of the second chapter to the end of the seventh chapter, this book was written in Aramaic, a Gentile language. But beginning with the eighth chapter Daniel again turned to the Hebrew, indicating that the remaining five chapters relate specifically to Israel.

We continue by reading verse two: *"And I saw in a vision; and it came to pass, when I saw, that I was at Shushan in the palace, which is in the province of Elam; and I saw in a vision, and I was by the river of Ulai."*

At the time that Daniel recieved the vision recorded in the eighth chapter, Shushan was the capital of the growing Medo-Persian Empire. It was about two hundred fifty miles due east from Babylon. It was built on a high hill with sides so steep that it could not be approached except by way of constructed roads, and these roads were guarded by heavy fortifications. According to Fausset, the Ulai was a small river that was formed by two streams that passed on either side of Shushan. The water from the Ulai was clear, clean, and good-tasting. Even when the Persians went out on battle campaigns, the nobles would carry with them water from the Ulai to drink. Only the old river bed is in evidence today. Earthquakes in that region probably closed the springs which fed the river. Shushan enjoyed much cooler weather than Babylon, and the royal family of Persia and the court usually spent their summers in Shushan and moved to Babylon in the winter. Both Nehemiah and Esther lived at Shushan (Est. 1:2; Neh. 1:1).

As the Babylonian Empire began to decline, the Medes and Persians revolted, and as we have previously declared, moved westward and challenged the Babylonian Empire by laying seige to Babylon itself. Due to the fact that siege of cities by ancient armies often lasted months, and possibly years, we can safely conclude that Babylon was under siege at the time Daniel was given the vision spoken of in Daniel 8:2. God revealed to him what the outcome of this struggle would be, and even showed him the course of history for the next two hundred years, and how these events would affect Israel, even to the bringing in of the kingdom promised in the covenants. Daniel said that for this revelation he was transported to Shushan by the River Ulai. We do not conclude that the prophet was transported bodily, but rather in the spirit.

Such spiritual projections in time and space are quite common in the Bible and should not be questioned, because after all, God who reveals secrets to men is also the author of both time and eternity. For example, we read in Revelation 1:9-10: *"I John, who also am your brother, and companion in tribulation, and in the kingdom and patience of Jesus Christ, was in the isle that is called Patmos, for the word of God, and for the testimony of Jesus Christ. I was in the Spirit on the Lord's day, and heard behind me a great voice, as of a trumpet."* Most commentaries interpret this scripture to mean that John was in spiritual communion with the Lord on Sunday, but this is not what it means at all. It means that the apostle was transported by the Holy Spirit forward into the day of the Lord, which begins with the tribulation period. Likewise, Daniel was taken in the spirit to the capital of the Medo-Persian Empire. He had no trouble getting by the guards, because no one could see him.

We continue now and read Daniel 8:3-8: *"Then I lifted up mine eyes, and saw, and, behold, there stood before the river a ram which had two horns: and the two horns were high; but one was higher than the other, and the higher came up last. I saw the ram pushing westward, and northward, and southward; so that no beasts might stand before him, neither was there any that could deliver out of his hand; but he did according to his will, and became great. And as I was considering, behold, an he goat came from the west on the face of the whole earth, and touched not the ground: and the goat had a notable horn between his eyes. And he came to the ram that had two horns, which I had seen standing before the river, and run unto him in the fury of his power. And I saw him come close unto the ram, and he was moved with choler against him, and smote the ram, and brake his two horns: and there was no power in the ram to stand before him, but he cast him down to the ground, and stamped upon him: and there was none that could deliver the ram out of his hand. Therefore the he goat waxed very great: and when he was strong, the great horn was broken; and for it came up four notable ones toward the four winds of heaven."*

Like the seventh chapter, the eighth chapter of Daniel is also most difficult to understand unless we make a firm connection to the end of the age and the return of the Lord Jesus Christ. Because many fail to make this connection, there is much speculation and misinterpretation by many ministers when they attempt to teach this chapter. What we are dealing with here is horns. The beasts on which these horns appear are of secondary importance. Horns are symbolic of kings and rulers, and the eighth chapter deals not so much with empires and governmental administration as it does with the identification and nature of notable potentates who would rule over the earth until Christ comes again.

We have no trouble at all with the vision as far as it pertains to the ram and the he goat. Even a child should be able to interpret it from the explanation given to Daniel by the archangel Gabriel. According to verse twenty, the ram represented the united kingdom of Media and Persia. The two horns on the ram represent the first two kings of this empire. We read "The ram which thou sawest having two horns are the kings of Media and Persia." As depicted by the ram, Medo-Persia moved westward and conquered Babylon; it moved southward to Egypt; and it moved northward to Greece. This was the extent of the Medo-Persian conquests. The two horns on the ram spoke of the two most notable kings of the dual empire. One horn came up on the ram, and then another horn came up which overshadowed the first.

The first horn represented Darius the Mede, and although Darius was a relatively good man, as far as ancient monarchs could be called good, he was not a strong king. He relied heavily on his three presidents and his prime minister, Daniel, for advice and counsel. His reign was also brief, lasting only two years. The second king of Medo-Persia, Cyrus, completely overshadowed Darius. Cyrus was the conqueror, the strong man, and we know that he ruled the kingdom for at least twenty years, and possibly longer. Therefore, we have no difficulty in determining that the ram is Medo-Persia. The short horn on the ram is Darius and the long horn on the ram is Cyrus. The agnostic or atheist might say that this was no big deal — that Daniel would have known at that time that Babylon would be defeated by the Medes and Persians, and as Darius and Cyrus were both leaders of their own countries, they would be the new rulers over the kingdom. However, in this same vision God showed Daniel that two hundred years in the future the Medo-Persian Empire would be overrun by Greece.

As Daniel watched the ram moving to the west, the east, and the north, a great male goat came charging in from the west in great fury, and the goat had a notable horn between his eyes. Daniel writes that the goat ran at the ram with all its power and with choler. *Choler* means "fierce anger." Again we are informed in the interpretation in verse twenty-one that the goat is Greece. The emblem of both the ram and the goat was in accordance with the nations they represented. The national emblem of Persia was a ram, and Persian coins had a ram's head engraved on one side. The national emblem of Greece was a goat and the coins of this nation carried the outline of a goat. The ancient capital of Greece was Aegae, which meant "the goat city." Alexander himself was nicknamed "The Goat," and his son by Roxana was called Aegus, "the son of a goat." Inasmuch as these two nations are so clearly identified by their national emblems, we should also expect the beasts of Daniel chapter seven to relate to nations with similar emblems — namely, England, the United States, Russia, the Afro-Asian bloc, and the Revived Roman Empire.

The fierce anger of the goat also points to Alexander, as Josephus records the Grecian emperor often went into a rage when he was defied or if battle plans did not develop as he expected. Daniel points out in verse six that the goat ran into the ram with great fury, and the battle of Salamis where the huge Medo-Persian army suffered a humiliating defeat at the hands of Alexander was one of the bloodiest and most bitter battles in all history. This battle, for all practical purposes, determined the history of the Middle East for the next two hundred years. The swiftness with which the goat charged is also indicative of the speed and great maneuverability of Alexander's legions. In verse eight we are informed that the goat grew great and strong, but as it reached the height of its power, the great horn on its head was broken. History records that Alexander died just after he had conquered all the civilized world in his day, and he was only thirty-three years of age. Verse eight states that after the great horn was broken, four other horns grew up in its place. After Alexander's death, his four generals divided the empire into four divisions, with each taking a province for his own dominion. Cassander took over Macedonia and Greece; Lysimachus claimed Asia Minor (Thrace and Bithynia); Seleucus took Syria and Babylonia; and Ptolemy took Egypt and North Africa.

The so-called higher critics of the Bible try to explain away this part of Daniel's prophecy by contending the entire book was not written until several hundred years after the Babylonian captivity; however, Josephus completely refutes this by telling us that Alexander read the prophecies which Daniel had written about him many years before in Babylon. For this reason, Alexander acknowledged the God of Israel and dealt kindly with the Jews. No one has ever successfully challenged the prophecies made by Daniel, and history proves them correct in every detail.

For many, Daniel 8:9-14 is difficult to understand. Before we attempt an explanation, let us read the passage: *"And out of one of them came forth a little horn, which waxed exceeding great, toward the south, and toward the east, and toward the pleasant land. And it waxed great, even to the host of heaven; and it cast down some of the host and of the stars to the ground, and stamped upon them. Yea, he magnified himself even to the prince of the host, and by him the daily sacrifice was taken away, and the place of his sanctuary was cast down. And an host was given him against the daily sacrifice by reason of transgression, and it cast down the truth to the ground; and it practised, and prospered. Then I heard one saint speaking, and another saint said unto that certain saint which spake, How long shall be the vision concerning the daily sacrifice, and the transgression of desolation, to give both the sanctuary and the host to be trodden under foot? And he said unto me, Unto two thousand and three hundred days; then shall the sanctuary be cleansed."*

There is a great division among Bible expositors as to the identity of the little horn of the eighth chapter of Daniel. Many believe that this prophecy was fulfilled when Antiochus Epiphanes, the governor of Syria, took Jerusalem and defiled the temple by offering a sow upon the altar. There is a great similarity between the little horn of chapter eight and Antiochus Epiphanes. The antiochus, or ruler of Syria, who preceded Epiphanes was the grandfather of Seleucus, the Grecian general. This antiochus died, and his brother Epiphanes became the new king to carry on the Syrian dynasty established by General Seleucus. We read in verse nine: *"And out of one of them* [doubtless meaning Seleucus], *came forth a little horn. . . ."*

Antiochus Epiphanes did offer an initial fulfillment of Daniel's prophecy. In our studies about this man from *The History of the Jews* by Josephus, we find that he was without a doubt the most despicable man in the world. He was a confirmed liar. He used the women in his own household as pawns to gain political favor. He tried to unify the four divisions of the old Grecian Empire, but he was turned back at Egypt when the Romans began to advance into that part of the world. Antiochus dealt unmercifully with the Jews. He killed anyone who possessed a copy of the Law of Moses, and he crucified one hundred thousand in Jerusalem who refused to worship his false gods. He hung all the young Jewish boys who had been circumcised; he horribly mutilated the Jewish women; and he offered a sow upon the altar in the temple. Josephus considered this deed the abomination of desolation prophesied by Daniel. The Jews, under the leadership of Judah the Maccabee, threw off the Syrian yoke and cleansed the temple. This was in the Jewish month of Kislev, the twenty-fifth day; this date corresponds to December 25, or Christmas. The day that the temple was cleansed and the perpetual lamp was lit has since been observed by the Jews as Hanukkah, the Feast of Lights.

In spite of the fact that those things which Antiochus Epiphanes did seemed to have satisfied the prophecy about the little horn of Daniel chapter eight, he was not the man depicted in the vision. Even those who make the application do so with great uncertainty. In almost every commentary on chapter eight that makes the connection to Antiochus Epiphanes, it is explained that he could possibly have been the little horn, or that the author is uncertain. Martin Luther said: *"This chapter in Daniel refers to both Antiochus and Antichrist."* The majority seem to concur with Luther's opinion — the prophecy was fulfilled in type in Antiochus, but the real little horn will be the Antichrist. In other words, the little horn of chapter eight that grew up out of one of the four notable horns is the same little horn of chapter seven who comes up in the middle of the ten horns on the head of the terrible beast. How can we be sure of this?

1. The four horns first point toward the four winds of heaven, indicating an end-time application.
2. It will be in the latter time when the transgressors are come to the full (v. 23).
3. The little horn shall be mighty by an alien power (v. 24). Antiochus Epiphanes used his own army.
4. He shall cause crafts to prosper (v. 25).
5. He shall stand up against the Prince of princes, the Lord Jesus Christ. Antiochus never came face-to-face with Jesus Christ. The exact meaning of Antichrist is the person who will stand up against the true Christ.
6. The little horn will be broken without hand. Although Antiochus Epiphanes was not killed in battle, his battle losses in Jerusalem and

Persia threw him into such a fit of depression that he could not eat and he died.

7. Jesus said that the abomination of desolation would occur during the tribulation.

Therefore, the aforementioned points prove conclusively that the little horn of chapter eight is the same little horn of chapter seven — the Antichrist. Let us keep in mind that in Daniel chapter eight, God revealed to the prophet the identity of world rulers to come — rulers that would change the history of the world in its relationship to Israel. How could a man today from the ancient Seleucus Syrian dynasty become the ruler over the Revived Roman Empire which we see taking shape in Europe today under the umbrella of the European Common Market? Let us not hedge on this point, because Daniel said the little horn, meaning the Antichrist, would come from the lineage of one of Alexander's four generals.

Fausset's Encyclopedia identifies ancient Assyria as generally that region which lies west of the Euphrates. This area would include the present nation of Syria. The Antichrist in several scriptures is said to be of Assyrian descent. For example, we read in Micah 5:5: *"And this man* [the Lord] *shall be the peace, when the Assyrian shall come into our land: and when he shall tread in our palaces. . . ."*

Once again we pose the question: How could a man identified as a Syrian, nationally, and a Greek, racially, become the head of the Revived Roman

Empire of Europe?

The great need for the growing industrial complex of Europe is oil. This is the one commodity they are short of. Therefore, a man from a Common Market nation, with a national connection to the oil-rich Arab nations, would be the ideal man to become president of the Common Market, which will be identified with the Revived Roman Empire. Thus, we see how a descendant of the Seleucian royal dynasty of Syria could easily become the ruler of the Revived Roman Empire.

We have always had a problem with the interpretation of Daniel 7:8 because we have been presented with the proposition of the little horn, the Antichrist, plucking up three of the ten horns of the beast kingdom, leaving only seven nations. Yet, according to chapter two, this last empire will have ten kings over it when Christ returns. The possible explanation would be that the Antichrist will kill three of the rulers and replace them with men of his own choosing, or that there would be thirteen nations within the beast kingdom, and the Antichrist will exclude three nations, leaving the ten mentioned. Therefore, before the ten kings, three other kings within the kingdom would be cast out by the Antichrist.

In our study of chapter eight we have progressed through verse fourteen. However, there are still many mysteries in verses nine through fourteen that we need to clear up.

In studying prophecy it is important to keep in

mind that the prophets of Israel knew nothing about the dispensation of grace. It was hidden from their prophetic view. Therefore, the course of prophetic events concerning the Kingdom Age will skip over the dispensation of grace just as if it would never occur. This truth is explained by Paul in Ephesians 3:2-5: *"If ye have heard of the dispensation of the grace of God which is given me to you-ward . . . Which in other ages was not made known unto the sons of men, as it is now revealed unto his holy apostles and prophets by the Spirit."*

Let us consider a verse-by-verse study of Daniel 8:9-14.

Verse 9: We notice in this verse that the direction of conquest by Antichrist is described. From the central starting point in his kingdom, he will move toward the south, then he will turn eastward toward the pleasant land, or Israel. This could not apply to Antiochus Epiphanes, because he moved southward out of Syria and then turned westward toward Jerusalem. This route of conquest would indicate that the Antichrist will move southward into Egypt and Libya from Europe, and then turn eastward and move against Jerusalem.

Verse 10: We are told in this verse that the power of the Antichrist will extend even into the heavens, and that he will even cast down some of the angels to the earth. It is quite understandable that the Antichrist will have a mighty array of powerful missiles and spaceships at his disposal. While we do not know exactly the nature of this conflict between the forces of Antichrist and the angels of God, it falls within the scope of the conflict described in Revelation 12:7: *"And there was war in heaven: Michael and his angels fought against the dragon; and the dragon fought and his angels."*

Verses 11 and 12: In these two verses we are informed that the power of Antichrist will be magnified, even to Michael, the prince of the heavenly host. Then the daily sacrifice in the temple that the Jews will rebuild in Jerusalem will be taken away. This will be when the Antichrist breaks his covenant with the Jews and then sits in the temple and declares to the whole world that he is God. The Jews are certainly looking forward to the resuming of animal sacrifices in the temple when it is built again. In Israel today young Jewish boys who can trace their ancestry back to the tribe of Levi are being sent to school to learn the order of temple worship and how to offer up to God the various sacrifices demanded by the law.

Verses 13 and 14: In these verses Daniel is prophetically tuned in to the conversation of two saints talking about the terrible blasphemy of the Antichrist in breaking his covenant with Israel; taking absolute control of Jerusalem; literally treading down the city with the feet of his army; stopping the daily sacrifices; and then sitting in the temple to declare himself to be the Messiah. We are not told who these certain saints are by Daniel, but they are without doubt the two witnesses of God who will be identified in Revelation 11:1-3: *"And there was given me a reed like unto a rod: and the angel stood, saying, Rise, and measure the temple of God, and the altar, and them that worship therein. But the court which is without the temple leave out, and measure it not; for it is given unto the Gentiles: and the holy city shall they tread under foot forty and two months. And I will give power unto my two witnesses, and they shall prophesy a thousand two hundred and threescore days, clothed in sackcloth."*

When referring to Gentile domination of Jerusalem during the last half of the tribulation, the period is given as forty-two months, but the period of the two supernatural Hebrew witnesses, whom we believe will be Moses and Elijah, will be twelve hundred sixty days. There are three hundred sixty-five days in our present Gentile calendar, and this would mean that from the time Antichrist orders his army to take over Jerusalem, it will be twelve hundred seventy-seven and a half days until Christ returns to deliver Jerusalem from his power. The two witnesses will be killed at the end of twelve hundred sixty days, which means their ministry will come to an end seventeen and a half days before Christ returns. However, we are informed in Daniel 8:14 that from the time that Antichrist commits the abomination of desolation and defiles the temple, until the sanctuary is cleansed, will be twenty-three hundred days. There have been various explanations for this time period. Some contend that the word used for days in the Hebrew text means mornings and evenings, or in other words, the Antichrist would make twenty-three hundred appearances in the temple (once in the morning and once in the evening) to show the whole world that he is God. If this be the case, then by an international television hookup, the Antichrist would appear on television at 6:00 a.m. and again at 6:00 p.m., from the temple in Jerusalem. This would be for eleven hundred fifty days. This would be ninety days before the two witnesses are killed, and it could be that they would have something to do with his failing to appear in the temple the next day, and this is why he kills them. If these twenty-three hundred days are complete twenty-four hour days, then the cleansing of the temple will not occur until almost three and a half years after Christ returns, and the rededication service would be in the temple that Christ will build, the Millennial Temple.

We have already discussed verses fifteen through twenty-two in conjunction with the explanation of that part of the vision which applied to the Medo-Persian and Grecian Empires; therefore, let us continue reading from verse twenty-three: *"And in the latter time of their kingdom, when the transgressors are come to the full, a king of fierce countenance, and understanding dark sentences, shall stand up. And his power shall be mighty, but not by his own power; and he shall destroy wonderfully, and shall prosper, and practise, and shall destroy the mighty and the holy people. And through his policy also he shall cause craft to prosper in his hand; and he shall magnify himself in his heart, and by peace shall destroy many: he shall also stand up against the Prince of princes; but he shall be broken without hand. And the vision of the evening and the morning which was told is true: wherefore shut thou up the vision; for it shall be for many days. And I Daniel fainted, and was sick certain days; afterward I rose up, and did the king's business; and I was astonished at the vision, but none understood it"* (Dan. 8:23-27).

We have here a more detailed description of the little horn of chapters seven and eight — the Antichrist will assume control over a ten-nation federated kingdom. For two hundred years Bible scholars have been predicting that Europe would unite and produce the Antichrist. Even when Europe was divided and fighting the bloodiest war that the world had ever known to that time, Walter Scott in his commentary on Revelation chapters seventeen and eighteen wrote that ten kings would arise in the last days out of Europe. In his commentary on Daniel, copyrighted in 1929, Clarence Larkin wrote that the fourth beast of Daniel chapter seven was the Revived Roman Empire of Europe, and the little horn would be the Antichrist. In his commentary on Daniel, copyrighted 1911, Dr. A.C. Gaebelein wrote:

"What then will come yet upon the territory of the Roman Empire? The empire will be revived (in ten nations) and established once more. . . .

We see indications of this already. . . . The Roman Empire has to be revived and then the ten kingdoms come into existence."

In the Pilgrim Bible, a footnote prepared in 1945 declares that the Roman Empire must be revived again in the form of a ten-nation empire. Even when Europe was divided and fighting in 1914, Bible scholars were writing that Europe would one day be united in ten nations. In World War II when England and France were fighting Italy and Germany, Bible scholars were writing that Europe would be united. Even when it seemed that it could never happen, fundamental pre-millennial men of God were saying that according to the Bible, it had to happen.

We are informed in Daniel chapter eight that the Antichrist would be mighty, but not by his power. He would march southward across the Mediterranean and take North Africa, and then turn eastward toward Jerusalem. He would claim to be a man of peace, and by peace destroy many. He would also be a man of industry and crafts — he will cause a great business boom in the world, and especially within his own ten-nation kingdom.

Europe is united today in a federated kingdom. It is united under the motto of peace and prosperity. In nearly all European nations, cars carry stickers on their windshields with "EU," standing for "Europe Unite."

On March 11, 1963, some twenty-five years ago,

we brought a message on the Common Market. Quoting that message:

> "*A new empire is rising in the world — an empire forged out of the western division of the Old Roman Empire. If the Common Market continues to grow in economic and political prominence, which it now appears it will, it may destroy both the political and economic influence of Britain and the United States, and both . . . could possibly be reduced to colonies of the EEC. . . . While the Common Market is controlled by a central committee, we should have no illusions. Charles DeGaulle, of France, is the ruling potentate, and he holds very definite visions of becoming a powerful world leader. By playing the East against the West, the general hopes to rise above both. . . . As we observe the Common Market of Europe with all its potential military, economic, political, and religious power, it certainly has all the characteristics of being the prophetic fulfillment of the Revived Roman Empire to be resurrected during the years just preceding our Lord's return. We think it will be extremely interesting to observe in the days to come, and see if further developments justify the conclusions that Bible students are reaching, concerning the rise of the Antichrist kingdom.*"

In 1992, Europe is to become one empire.

Chapter Nine

Chapter nine of the book of Daniel stands out as the paragon of Bible prophecy. This chapter proves beyond a shadow of a doubt that God revealed the future course of world events to faithful men of God, and they wrote about things to come as they were led by the Holy Spirit. Dr. H.A. Ironside called the ninth chapter of Daniel *"the greatest-of-all-time prophecies."* Sir Edward Denny called it *"the backbone of prophecy."* The prophecy recorded in this chapter proves that Jesus Christ is the Messiah of Israel. Chapter eight tells about a little horn, the Antichrist, who will rise up in the last days to challenge the Christ of God. This little horn will magnify himself and command millions to be killed for failing to worship him as God. He will rule over a ten-nation kingdom, and gain control of the whole earth. The prophecy about the little horn began in chapter seven where his kingdom is described and its chronological appearance is given. Chapter eight describes his evil nature and his great power. Chapter nine tells about his deceitful dealings with the nation of Israel. Chapter nine also tells us about a greater horn than the little horn. This great horn will not be from the horn of the Syrian dynasty, but from the horn of David, the royal house of Israel. We read of Him in Psalm 132:17-18: *"There will I make the horn of David to bud: I have ordained a lamp for mine household. His enemies will I clothe with shame: but upon himself shall his crown flourish."* We read of Him again in Luke 1:68-70: *"Blessed by the Lord God of Israel; for he hath visited and redeemed his people, And hath raised up an horn of salvation for us in the house of his servant David; As he spake by the mouth of his holy prophets. . . . "* The prophecy of the seventy weeks of Daniel chapter nine tells how the horn of David, the Messiah of Israel, would be cut off from His people until the abomination of the little horn had run its course.

We begin our study by reading Daniel 9:1-2: *"In the first year of Darius the son of Ahasuerus, of the seed of the Medes, which was made king over the realm of the Chaldeans; In the first year of his reign I Daniel understood by books the number of the years, whereof the word of the Lord came to Jeremiah the prophet, that he would accomplish seventy years in the desolations of Jerusalem."*

The setting in time for chapter nine, as explained by Daniel, was in the first year of the reign of Darius over the province of Babylon. At this time Babylon had fallen to the Medes and the Persians. Darius is given as the son of Ahasuerus the Mede. Ahasuerus the Mede is not to be confused with Ahasuerus the Persian mentioned in Ezra 4:5 or the Persian Ahasuerus who was the king during the time of Esther. Ahasuerus was a common Mede and Persian name and there were several rulers with this name.

Later in order to eliminate the historical confusion, kings with the same name were assigned numbers (King Edward V, King Henry IV, etc.).

After the defeat of Babylon and the institution of a new government, Daniel begins to contemplate what effect this turn of events would have on the status of the Jews in the foreign country. The prophet began studying the books of Jeremiah. These books were not bound like our books today. They were scrolls of parchments, and all together, they composed the book of Jeremiah as it is in our Bible. Daniel could have commanded that the writings of Jeremiah from Jerusalem be brought to him in Babylon, because Daniel was next to Darius in authority. Daniel probably read first from Jeremiah 25:11: *"And this whole land shall be a desolation, and an astonishment; and these nations shall serve the king of Babylon seventy years."* But the prophet found hope for Israel in Jeremiah 29:10: *"For thus saith the Lord, That after seventy years be accomplished at Babylon I will visit you, and perform my good word toward you, in causing you to return to this place."*

As Daniel read the books by Jeremiah he understood that his fellow prophet wrote only as he himself did — by the word of the Lord. We read in 2 Timothy 3:16: *"All scripture is given by inspiration of God. . . ."* Also in 2 Peter 1:21: *"For the prophecy came not in old time by the will of man: but holy men of God spake as they were moved by the Holy Ghost."* Daniel was not so vain as to believe he had cornered the market on prophetic revelations. He accepted the prophecies of Jeremiah as also coming from the Lord, and according to Jeremiah, the time for God to look again upon His people, hear their cries, and deliver them from bondage had arrived. This promise for whoever names the name of the Lord is given in 2 Chronicles 7:14: *"If my people, which are called by my name, shall humble themselves, and pray, and seek my face, and turn from their wicked ways; then will I hear from heaven, and will forgive their sin, and will heal their land."*

We read next Daniel 9:3-4: *"And I set my face unto the Lord God, to seek by prayer and supplications, with fasting, and sackcloth, and ashes: And I prayed unto the Lord my God, and made my confession, and said, O Lord, the great and dreadful God, keeping the covenant, and mercy to them that love him, and to them that keep his commandment."*

When Daniel understood by the word of the Lord through Jeremiah that God would again look upon His people at the end of seventy years of bondage, he began to fast in sackcloth and ashes. Sackcloth and ashes indicated extreme self-abasement and need for God's mercy. After Daniel had emptied himself of all self-glory and self-righteousness, he sought the face of the Lord God by prayer. He ran after the Lord in prayer; he pursued the Lord to get His attention.

At the beginning of his prayer, Daniel made his confession, asking God to forgive his own sins and shortcomings. Although there is not a single sin or fault mentioned against Daniel in all the Bible, the prophet was careful not to fall into the error of the self-righteous. He claimed only that righteousness of God which is imputed by faith. Next, Daniel claimed the promises of God as the Almighty who always kept His word and showed mercy to those who love Him and keep His commandments.

After Daniel had pursued the Lord in prayer until he was assured of an audience, he submitted his petition. In his prayer we find the true basis for all Christian patriotism. *"We have sinned, and have committed iniquity, and have done wickedly, and have rebelled, even by departing from thy precepts and from thy judgments: Neither have we hearkened unto thy servants the prophets, which spake in thy name to our kings, our princes, and our fathers, and to all the people of the land. O Lord, righteousness belongeth unto thee, but unto us confusion of faces, as at this day; to the men of Judah, and to the inhabitants of Jerusalem, and unto all Israel, that are near, and that are far off, through all the countries whither thou hast driven them, because of their trespass that they have trespassed against thee. O Lord, to us belongeth confusion of face, to our kings, to our princes, and to our fathers, because we have sinned against thee. To the Lord our God belong mercies and forgiveness, though we have rebelled against him; Neither have we obeyed the voice of the Lord our God, to walk in his laws, which he set before us by his servants the prophets. Yea, all Israel have transgressed thy law, even by departing, that they might not obey thy voice; therefore the curse is poured upon us, and the oath that is written in the law of Moses the servant of God, because we have sinned against him. And he hath confirmed his words, which he spake against us, and against our judges that judged us, by bringing upon us a great evil: for under the whole heaven hath not been done as hath been done upon Jerusalem. As it is written in the law of Moses, all this evil is come upon us: yet made we not our prayer before the Lord our God, that we might turn from our iniquities, and understand thy truth. Therefore hath the Lord watched upon the evil, and brought it upon us: for the Lord our God is righteous in all his works which he doeth: for we obeyed not his voice"* (Dan. 9:5-14).

Daniel's prayer is in three main parts. The first part, which we have just quoted, concerns the reasons for Israel's trouble. Of course, God already knew all about it, but Daniel revealed to the Lord that he himself knew why his nation had been overrun by a foreign aggressor, hundreds of thousands of them killed, the young men operated on so they could produce no children, the women raped, and their cities plundered. Daniel said: "God, I know why it has happened!" Let us now consider these reasons for Israel's troubles, which Daniel gave.

1. As a nation Israel sinned and committed iniquity (reveled in adultery, fornication, and

sexual perversion).

2. Israel rebelled against God, departed from the precepts of God upon which the nation was founded, and said they would not be judged of the Lord, meaning they would not abide by God's ordinances for human government.

3. Israel mocked the prophets who tried to warn them to turn from their sins.

4. Because of the people's transgression, they had become confused as to their national mission. Nationally, they didn't know why they existed or where they were going.

5. And likewise the king, the governors, and the mayors became confused because the people were confused. They didn't know what the people wanted. It was war one day and peace the next. When Babylon invaded Israel the king would agree to a peace treaty one day, and then the next day he would break it.

6. According to verse 12, the greatest evil perpetrated upon the nation was by the judges from the high court right on down to the lower courts. They no longer judged according to God's moral law, but rather according to political expediency and their own greed.

7. Because the nation failed to heed the warning of the preachers and repent, God brought judgment upon them and Daniel declares that the people deserved no less than they received.

The second part of the body of Daniel's prayer for his nation is found in a single verse: *"And now, O Lord our God, that hast brought thy people forth out of the land of Egypt with a mighty hand, and hast gotten thee renown, as at this day; we have sinned, we have done wickedly"* (Dan. 9:15).

Throughout the Bible, Israel is reminded of their deliverance by God out of the hand of their oppressors in Egypt. They are continually reminded of this because God had a plan and purpose for saving them from bondage, and for this reason He saved them with mighty signs and wonders so that their children and their children's children would never forget to uphold that mission for which God saved them. God delivered them to form a holy and righteous nation so that they might testify of Him to the whole world, and be a blessing to all people.

We continue and read the last part of the prophet's prayer: *"O Lord, according to all thy righteousness, I beseech thee, let thine anger and thy fury be turned away from thy city Jerusalem, thy holy mountain: because for our sins, and for the iniquities of our fathers, Jerusalem and thy people are become a reproach to all that are about us. Now therefore, O our God, hear the prayer of thy servant, and his supplications, and cause thy face to shine upon thy sanctuary that is desolate, for the Lord's sake. O my God, incline thine ear, and hear; open thine eyes, and behold our desolations, and the city which is called by thy name: for we do not present our supplications before thee for our righteousnesses, but for thy great mercies. O Lord, hear; O Lord, forgive; O Lord, hearken and do; defer not, for thine own sake, O my God: for thy city and thy people are called by thy name"* (Dan. 9:16-19).

Over and over in the petition part of his prayer, Daniel pursued the Lord. He prayed: *"O Lord I beseech thee; O our God, hear; O my God, incline thine ear; O Lord, forgive; O Lord, hearken."* Some might wonder why this old Jew was so bothered. He was in his mid-eighties; he was the prime minister to King Darius; he had a fine palace with competent servants; and he had the finest food the kingdom could afford. Why didn't he just relax and enjoy retirement? The reason is that he loved his nation and he loved his people. He was a godly patriot, and he knew before his nation could be saved there would have to be forgiveness from God and a Heavensent revival.

We continue and read Daniel 9:20-23: *"And whiles I was speaking, and praying, and confessing my sin and the sin of my people Israel, and presenting my supplication before the Lord my God for the holy mountain of my God; Yea, whiles I was speaking in prayer, even the man Gabriel, whom I had seen in the vision at the beginning, being caused to fly swiftly, touched me about the time of the evening oblation. And he informed me, and talked with me, and said, O Daniel, I am now come forth to give thee skill and understanding. At the beginning of thy supplications the commandment came forth, and I am come to shew thee; for thou art greatly beloved: therefore understand the matter, and consider the vision."*

The power of Daniel's prayer is witnessed by the fact that God heard him at the very beginning and He knew exactly what Daniel would say in his prayer. We are told in Joel 2:28 that during the millennium, God will pour out His Spirit upon all flesh, and those who seek God and His will are to enjoy close and sweet communion with the Lord. We read of the millennium in Isaiah 65:24: *"And it shall come to pass, that before they call, I will answer; and while they are yet speaking, I will hear."* What happened to Daniel will be very commonplace during the Kingdom Age. People will bow their heads to pray and before they finish there will be an angel standing by them to answer their prayer.

This must have been a glorious experience for Daniel. Even before he had finished his prayer, the archangel Gabriel tapped him on the shoulder and informed the prophet that he had been commanded to fly swiftly to him. How fast is swiftly in heavenly language? We have no idea. Gabriel's flight to Daniel could not have taken over an hour because the Jewish oblation lasted from three to four in the afternoon. This was the time the priests in the temple offered the sacrifice on the altar. It is called the ninth hour in the Scriptures. The reason the sacrifice had to be offered during the ninth hour was because the animal sacrifice looked forward to the eternal sacrifice, Jesus Christ the Lamb of God. And it was in the ninth hour that Jesus Christ finished His atoning work on the cross and died for the sins of the world. We read in Matthew 27:45-46, 50: *"Now from the sixth hour there was darkness over all the land unto the ninth hour. And about the ninth hour Jesus cried with a loud voice, saying, Eli, Eli, lama sabachthani? that is to say, My God, my God, why hast thou forsaken me? . . . Jesus, when he had cried again with a loud voice, yielded up the ghost."*

As the sacrifice was being offered the priest would pray for the acceptance of the sacrifice for the sins of Israel, and they prayed for Israel to become holy and righteous in God's sight so that Messiah would come and bring in the kingdom promised in the covenants. Therefore, it was according to biblical instruction and Jewish tradition for Daniel to be praying at oblation time for God to forgive the sins of Israel and fulfill His promise according to the covenants. We read that Gabriel informed Daniel that he was sent to give him skill and understanding. This knowledge that Gabriel gave him concerned that which the prophet wanted to know: When would God take away Israel's transgression and fulfill the covenant? Gabriel said that he would give this information to Daniel because Daniel was greatly beloved, meaning that he was loved greatly by the Lord. Paul referred to Christians in the various churches as "beloved" throughout his epistles. He did not mean that they were beloved by him, although they were loved by him as much as man can love his brothers and sisters in Christ. He meant that they were beloved of God. Though it may mean a great deal to know you are the beloved of men, it means infinitely more to know that you are beloved of God.

We continue and read the message which Gabriel delivered to Daniel from God concerning the future of Israel. *"Seventy weeks are determined upon thy people and upon thy holy city, to finish the transgression, and to make an end of sins, and to make reconciliation for iniquity, and to bring in everlasting righteousness, and to seal up the vision and prophecy, and to anoint the most Holy. Know therefore and understand, that from the going forth of the commandment to restore and to build Jerusalem unto the Messiah the Prince shall be seven weeks, and threescore and two weeks: the street shall be built again, and the wall, even in troublous times. And after threescore and two weeks shall Messiah be cut off, but not for himself: and the people of the prince that shall come shall destroy the city and the sanctuary; and the end thereof shall be with a flood, and unto the end of the war desolations are determined. And he shall confirm the covenant with many for one week: and in the midst of the week he shall cause the sacrifice and the oblation to cease, and for the overspreading of abominations he shall make it desolate, even until the consummation, and that determined shall be poured upon the desolate"* (Dan. 9:24-27).

Gabriel informed Daniel that concerning Israel,

God had a seventy-week plan in operation. During this time period, all his prayers would be answered. This plan involved the following things which Daniel had mentioned:

1. Finish the transgression
2. Make an end of sin
3. Make reconciliation for iniquity
4. Bring in everlasting righteousness
5. Seal up the vision and prophecy
6. Anoint the most Holy

In considering the meaning of each of the six things which Gabriel prophesied, let us keep in mind that according to verse twenty-four, they concern Israel as a race, the holy city Jerusalem, the land of Palestine, and the temple. The prophecy is Jewish from beginning to end. Gentiles are not even referred to in an indirect way, and the dispensation of grace is completely hidden from view.

Point number one, *finish the transgression*, means the end of Israel's transgression against the law and the commandments of God. The transgressions of Israel will be finished when Christ returns to rule on David's throne. *"According to their uncleanness and according to their transgressions have I done unto them, and hid my face from them. Therefore thus saith the Lord God; Now will I bring again the captivity of Jacob, and have mercy upon the whole house of Israel, and will be jealous for my holy name"*

(Ezek. 39:24-25). *"Hearken unto me, my people; and give ear unto me, O my nation: for a law shall proceed from me, and I will make my judgment to rest for a light of the people"* (Isa. 51:4).

Point number two, *make an end of sin*. The end of sin is when the sinner accepts Christ as the One who died for sin, but the end of sin as mentioned by Gabriel meant the sins of Israel. Israel as a nation has not to this time accepted Christ as the promised Messiah; therefore, they continue in sin. This too will be accomplished when Christ returns and Israel receives Him as their sin bearer. *"And so all Israel shall be saved: as it is written, There shall come out of Sion the Deliverer, and shall turn away ungodliness from Jacob: For this is my covenant unto them, when I shall take away their sins"* (Rom. 11:26-27).

Point number three, *make reconciliation for iniquity*. Iniquity means wickedness and a sinful condition — lost in sin. *"But he was wounded for our transgressions, he was bruised for our iniquities: the chastisement of our peace was upon him; and with his stripes we are healed. All we like sheep have gone astray; we have turned every one to his own way; and the Lord hath laid on him the iniquity of us all"* (Isa. 53:5-6). A Jew can be saved today like any Gentile by accepting Christ as Savior. But the salvation of Israel as mentioned by Gabriel means the saving of the entire nation. This will occur when every living Jew looks upon Him whom they have pierced and mourns for Him even as an only Son (Zech. 12:12).

Point number four, *bring in everlasting righteousness*. No man, including the Jew, has any righteousness of his own. The only righteousness that man can attain is that righteousness which is by faith in Christ, and this is an imputed righteousness. Righteousness shall prevail in Israel when Christ is believed in as the Messiah. This truth is declared in Jeremiah 23:6: *"In his days Judah shall be saved, and Israel shall dwell safely: and this is his name whereby he shall be called, THE LORD OUR RIGHTEOUSNESS."*

Point number five, *seal up the vision and prophecy*. This does not mean the particular vision and prophecy which Gabriel delivered to Daniel. It means all visions and all prophecies recorded in the Bible. All the prophecies given in the Bible were revealed to Israelites, and all prophecy is sealed up in Israel. Daniel was commanded to seal up the book of his prophecy until the end, meaning when the Jew began to return to the land. And only when the Jews began to return to their land did men begin to understand the prophecies that applied to the last days. Gentile ministers today expound the prophecies which were given to the Jews, but the time is coming when Christ returns that the gift of prophecy and vision will again be sealed up in God's covenant people. We read in Joel 2:27-28: *"And ye* [Israel] *shall know that I am in the midst of Israel, and that I am the Lord your God . . . And it shall come to pass afterward, that I will pour out my spirit upon all flesh; and your sons and your daughters shall prophesy, your old men shall dream dreams, your young men shall see visions. "* Some churches today try to claim this promise for themselves, but it applies only to the sons and daughters of Israel during the millennium.

Point number six, *anoint the most Holy.* The anointing of the most Holy, or holy of holies, means the sanctification of the temple with the presence of Messiah. This will not occur until the Lord comes to His temple. We read of this glorious event in Ezekiel 43:2, 4-5: *"And, behold, the glory of the God of Israel came from the way of the east: and his voice was like a noise of many waters: and the earth shined with his glory. . . . And the glory of the Lord came into the house . . . and, behold, the glory of the Lord filled the house."*

All six of these things which Daniel prayed for will be fulfilled when Israel receives the Messiah. The hope of those things promised by God in the covenants lay in a Savior, a Redeemer, a Deliverer, the One whom the New Testament reveals as the Lord Jesus Christ. The Messiah will come to Israel at the end of the seventy prophetic weeks, but first He must be cut off for the sins of the world.

In Daniel 9:24 we read that Gabriel assured Daniel that God would bring an end to the transgressions of Israel; He would reconcile them unto Himself; He would bring everlasting righteousness upon the nation; He would commit to them His word for all nations; and He would anoint the temple with the presence of the blessed and holy Messiah. But all these things would not be accomplished until seventy weeks had expired. Of course, we look at Israel today and see that in the twenty-five hundred years since Gabriel gave the prophecy, the temple is not built; Israel continues in transgression; they not only cannot witness to all nations, they are fighting for their very existence; and we see no Messiah on the throne of David. What happened? Did Gabriel goof?

No indeed — Gabriel delivered the message just as God gave it to him, and it will come to pass just as the Bible declares. We have to interpret the seventy weeks according to the Hebrew accounting of time. *"After the number of the days in which ye searched the land, even forty days, each day for a year, shall ye bear your iniquities, even forty years, and ye shall know my breach of promise"* (Num. 14:34). God breached His promise to bring Israel into the promised land and make of them a holy nation with forty days, each day for a year. He breached His promise with forty years because of their iniquities and transgressions; therefore, they had to bear their transgressions forty years. By this same Hebrew accounting method, Gabriel informed Daniel that Israel would continue to bear their transgressions for four hundred ninety days, one day for a year, constituting a time period of four hundred ninety years. This method of accounting for time is most common in the Hebrew calendar. For example, we read in Genesis 29:15-18 that Jacob agreed to work for Rachel for "one week," and both he and Laban understood that he meant seven years — one year for each day. But in considering this time ratio, we must be very careful to keep it in its proper perspective, because it is used in relation to Israel, and Israel alone. It is never used to account for time for the Gentiles. Some try to use this method to account for the thirteen hundred days that Antichrist will desecrate the temple, the two divisions of the tribulation composed of forty-two months each, or the twenty-three hundred days of Daniel 8:14. They use these definite time periods given for tribulation events on the same year-for-a-day ratio, and they stretch them over the dispensation of grace to try to prove that all the prophecies concerning the tribulation and the millennium have already been fulfilled. But this method of time accounting is restricted to Israel and must never be applied to the Gentiles. When the year-for-a-day ratio is to be used, it is always indicated.

Thus we understand that according to the prophecy delivered by Gabriel to Daniel, God had appointed a time period of four hundred ninety years to bring in the kingdom and make Israel the head of all nations.

Of course, we understand that if this time period was to have begun immediately, then it would have ended in 46 B.C., long before the birth of the promised Messiah. To clarify when the seventy weeks were to begin and when they were to end, let us go back and read again Daniel 9:24-25: *"Seventy weeks are determined upon thy people and upon thy holy city, to finish the transgression, and to make an end of sins,* *and to make reconciliation for iniquity, and to bring in everlasting righteousness, and to seal up the vision and prophecy, and to anoint the most Holy. Know therefore and understand, that from the **going forth of the commandment to restore and to build Jerusalem unto the Messiah the Prince** shall be seven weeks, and threescore and two weeks: the street shall be built again, and the wall, even in troublous times."*

According to the prophecy, this time period of four hundred ninety years was not to begin until a command was issued to rebuild Jerusalem. There were four separate decrees issued by Persian and Median kings concerning the rebuilding of the temple and the rebuilding of Jerusalem. The first decree is mentioned in Ezra 1:1-2: *"Now in the first year of Cyrus king of Persia, that the word of the Lord by the mouth of Jeremiah might be fulfilled, the Lord stirred up the spirit of Cyrus king of Persia, that he made a proclamation throughout all his kingdom, and put it also in writing, saying, Thus saith Cyrus king of Persia, The Lord God of heaven hath given me all the kingdoms of the earth; and he hath charged me to build him an house at Jerusalem, which is in Judah."*

This first decree was issued by Cyrus in 536 B.C. However, we note this decree was to fulfill Jeremiah's prophecy that after seventy years Jews would begin to return to the land. We also note that this decree related only to the rebuilding of the temple; it did not permit the rebuilding of Jerusalem, and Gabriel said the four hundred ninety years were to begin with the commandment to rebuild the Holy City. Therefore, we must look for a subsequent decree.

Another decree was issued by Darius the Mede in 519 B.C. We read in Ezra chapter five that the authority of the Jews to go back and rebuild the temple was questioned. So Darius made a search of the treasure house, which also held the official state documents, and he found the parchment upon which Cyrus had recorded the first decree seventeen years previously. And so Darius made his own decree to show that he favored the first decree, and he also enlarged upon the first decree concerning the architectural design of the temple so that the Jews would not again be interfered with in their construction. But this second decree concerned only the rebuilding of the temple, and so we must continue to search for the starting place for the four hundred ninety years.

A third decree was issued forty-two years after the second decree by King Artaxerxes of Persia. The third decree, as we read in Ezra chapter seven, permitted the Jewish priests and Levites to return to Jerusalem for the reinstitution of temple services. It also provided for funds to be drawn from the Persian treasury to purchase necessary supplies for the temple, including animal sacrifices. We read in Ezra 7:16-17 that the king and his counsellors considered the money a freewill offering to the God of Israel. They did not expect it to be repaid. But again we note that this third decree still related only to the temple; therefore, we must look for still another decree.

We read of the fourth decree in Nehemiah chapter two. In verses one and two we read that Nehemiah, the king's cupbearer, appeared before Artaxerxes with a sad countenance. The king was quite concerned and asked if he were sick. It was not Nehemiah's health which concerned Artaxerxes, but rather his own, because the cupbearer had to taste the king's wine first to see if it were poisoned. Nehemiah explained to Artaxerxes the reason for his sadness in verse three: *"Why should not my countenance be sad, when the city, the place of my fathers' sepulchres, lieth waste, and the gates thereof are consumed with fire?"* We read in verse four that the king then gave Nehemiah a letter to the keeper of the forest to provide timber for the rebuilding of the wall and part of the city. This was in 445 B.C., and from the moment that Artaxerxes signed the letter, the four hundred ninety years began to expire. We note in Daniel 9:25 that because the wall would be rebuilt in troublesome times, its construction would take seven weeks. This period would amount to forty-nine years. Ezra and Nehemiah wrote of the great difficulties encountered, and we read this account in *The History of the Jews* by Josephus:

> *". . . When the Ammonites, and Moabites, and Samaritans . . . heard that the building went on apace, they took it heinously, and proceeded to lay snares for them, and to hinder their intentions. They also slew many of the Jews, and*

sought how they might destroy Nehemiah himself, by hiring some foreigners to kill him. They also put the Jews in fear, and disturbed them, and spread abroad rumours, as if many nations were ready to make an expedition against them, by which they were harassed, and almost left off the building. But none of these things could deter Nehemiah from being diligent about the work."

Josephus went on to write that Nehemiah made the workmen labor with their armor on. They had to wear their swords at all times with their shields within a few feet. A trumpeter was stationed every five hundred feet around the city to sound the alarm when the enemies attacked. Finally, after forty-nine troublesome and agonizing years, the rebuilding of the wall and the city was completed.

We notice in Daniel 9:25 that from the signing of the decree to rebuild Jerusalem to the Messiah would be sixty-nine of the seventy weeks, or four hundred eighty-three years. This verse does not indicate whether the conception, birth, baptism, or crucifixion of Jesus is meant. In verse twenty-six Gabriel noted that from the completion of the contruction of Jerusalem to the cutting off of Messiah would be sixty-two weeks, add to this the seven weeks of rebuilding the city, and we arrive at the conclusion that the end of the sixty-ninth week would come at the time Christ would be nailed to the cross.

It is agreed by the vast majority of biblical

authorities that Christ was crucified at the age of thirty-three and a half years. Therefore, it occurred in 34 A.D. It has been discovered, and widely reported in thousands of reliable publications, that an error was made by the Romans of four years in setting up their calendar, the same calendar system we use today. This was a plus factor, therefore we have to add to the thirty-four years, four more years. We then subtract from the sixty-nine weeks, four hundred eighty-three years, the sum of thirty-four years and four years, and we arrive at four hundred forty-five years. Artaxerxes signed the decree to rebuild Jerusalem in 445 B.C., proving beyond any reasonable doubt that Jesus Christ is the Messiah of Israel. The Messiah had to be cut off in 34 A.D., and Christ is the only person who history records as claiming to be this Promised One. The only reference that Josephus made to Jesus Christ was in chapter three, book eighteen, of his *History of the Jews*. We quote:

> *"Now there was about this time Jesus, a wise man, if it be lawful to call him a man; for he was a doer of wonderful works, a teacher of such men as receive the truth with pleasure. He drew over to him both many of the Jews and many of the Gentiles. He was Christ. And when Pilate, at the suggestion of the principal men amongst us, had condemned him to the cross, those that loved him at the first did not forsake him; for he appeared to them alive again the third day; as the divine*

prophets had foretold these and ten thousand other wonderful things concerning him."

We read in Daniel 9:26: *"And after threescore and two weeks shall Messiah be cut off, but not for himself. . . ."* What did Gabriel mean? We read in John 18:38: *"Pilate saith unto him, What is truth? And when he had said this, he went out again unto the Jews, and saith unto them, I find in him no fault at all."* Jesus was innocent. He died not for Himself, but for the sins of the world (1 Cor. 15:3).

We have just studied the first two divisions of Daniel's seventy prophetic weeks. We call these Daniel's seventy prophetic weeks, but they would be better named Gabriel's seventy prophetic weeks.

What did Gabriel say would happen after the Messiah would be cut off? We read again in Daniel 9:26: *". . . and the people of the prince that shall come shall destroy the city and the sanctuary. . . ."* In other words, Gabriel told Daniel that after the Messiah would be cut off from his people Israel, Jerusalem and the temple would be destroyed. Why would the Holy City and the temple be destroyed after the Messiah was cut off? Because of sin, and the people refused to accept Jesus Christ as the One who would end their transgressions and take away their sin as Daniel had prayed. In the Temple Discourse, Matthew chapter twenty-three, Jesus pulled no punches. He layed the sins of Israel bare, in language that no minister of the gospel has ever dared use to expose the sins of his nation. Jesus said of Israel in Matthew 23:33: *"Ye serpents, ye generation of vipers, how can ye escape the damnation of hell?"* When Jesus left the temple after delivering a hell-fire message to sinning Israel, His disciples followed Him. They were probably trying to placate Jesus, cool Him down a bit perhaps, and they pointed out to Him the beauty of the temple. It would appear they were trying to show Him that there was something good and beautiful left in Israel — that there was something worth saving. But Jesus would not be placated. He said of the temple in Matthew 24:2: *". . . I say unto you, There shall not be left here one stone upon another, that shall not be thrown down."*

After the Messiah was crucified, the city and the temple were destroyed just as prophesied. They were destroyed as Gabriel declared — because Israel cut off their own Messiah. Now who would be the agent of destruction? *". . . The people of the prince that shall come shall destroy the city and the sanctuary . . ."* (Dan. 9:26).

Let us note carefully the wording of this prophecy. The people of the prince, not the prince himself, shall destroy the city and the sanctuary. Josephus, who was a captive of the Roman army besieging Jerusalem, wrote that after the death of Nero, General Galba was recalled to be made emperor. But a conspiracy that opposed him developed and he was assassinated. After Galba, Ortho was made emperor, but he was incapable of ruling and, like Nero, he committed suicide. There followed a period of revolution and political instability, and finally, the general in command of the Israeli expedition was recalled to restore order and become emperor. This man was General Vespasian, the father of Captain Titus. When Vespasian left for Rome, he made his son Titus general, and he was put in command of the army besieging Jerusalem. Just a few days before the final assault on Jerusalem, Vespasian was crowned emperor of the Roman Empire, making Titus a prince. Therefore, the army which destroyed Jerusalem and the temple was commanded by a prince, just as prophesied in Daniel 9:26. But also as prophesied, Titus did everything he possibly could to spare the buildings of the city and the temple. He had issued orders that the city and the temple be saved as much as possible, but his well-trained and disciplined army, for some unexplained reason, went berserk and pillaged and burned the city and the temple. Titus intervened personally at the temple itself to save it, but the soldiers, according to Josephus, were seized by a divine urge and refused to heed the hand signs or voice of Titus. Thus, Jerusalem and the temple were destroyed by the people of the prince. This was a remarkable demonstration of a prophecy being fulfilled even to the most minute detail.

Notice in Daniel 9:26 that there is no mention at any time of the four hundred ninety years being consumed from the cutting off of Messiah to the destruction of the temple. The reason for this is when the Messiah was cut off, God stopped the clock. This was the iniquity that caused God to breach His promise of four hundred ninety years to the bringing in of the kingdom. The time stopped at the end of the sixty-ninth week, and it has not started again to this day. There is still one week of the seventy prophetic weeks to be fulfilled. This period of time that has been going on from the end of the sixty-ninth week to the time it begins in the seventieth week is called a gap, and this particular gap is the dispensation of grace. God calls it a breach in His promise to Israel. We read in Numbers 14:34: *"After the number of the days in which ye searched the land, even forty days, each day for a year, shall ye bear your iniquities, even forty years, and ye shall know my breach of promise."*

It was quite common a few decades ago, and still happens occasionally, for a woman to sue a man for breach of promise. The man would promise to marry a woman, and for one reason or another, he would not show up for the wedding. The jilted bride would sue the man for breach in his promise, and she would bring suit for real and personal damages. This is where it comes from — from God breaching His promise to His faithless wife, Israel. We should remember that God does not breach His promise without good cause. We read in Isaiah 30:13: *"Therefore this iniquity shall be to you as a breach ready to fall, swelling out in a high wall, whose breaking cometh suddenly at an instant."* The instant Israel crucified the Son of God, the iniquity was so great God not only turned away from His only begotten Son as the sins of the world were laid upon Him, but He also turned His face away from His covenant people who were responsible. The clock ticking off the time on the seventy prophetic weeks was stopped just as if you would pull the plug on your electric clock.

But let us keep in mind that the promise which God made to Israel has only been breached, it has not been cancelled. Everything that God has said he would do from the creation of the world will be done. But because of Israel's iniquity, salvation has come to the Gentiles during the breach. We read in Romans 11:30: *"For ye [Gentiles] in times past have not believed God, yet have now obtained mercy through their [Israel's] unbelief."*

We read also in Roman 11:26: *"And so all Israel shall be saved: as it is written, There shall come out of Sion the Deliverer, and shall turn away ungodliness from Jacob."* When will the breach be healed and the time begin again on Daniel's seventieth and last prophetic week? The Word of God tells us in Isaiah 30:25-26: *"And there shall be upon every high mountain, and upon every high hill, rivers and streams of waters in the day of the great slaughter, when the towers fall. Moreover the light of the moon shall be as the light of the sun, and the light of the sun shall be sevenfold, as the light of seven days, in the day that the Lord bindeth up the breach of his people. . . ."* The breach will be closed and time on the last week resumed when the tribulation period begins.

We read again in Daniel 9:26: *". . . and the end thereof shall be with a flood. . . ."* What end? The end of the seventy weeks — the last week — the tribulation period. We read on: *". . . and unto the end of the war desolations are determined."* We get a closer view of the desolations which are coming upon the world and wars the likes of which men have never seen to this time. Jesus said of this time of war, pestilence, and famine: *"When ye therefore shall see the abomination of desolation, spoken of by Daniel the prophet, stand in the holy place, (whoso readeth, let him understand:) Then let them which be in Judaea flee into the mountains. . . . For then shall be great tribulation, such as was not since the beginning of the world to this time, no, nor ever shall be. And except those days should be shortened, there should no flesh be saved . . ."* (Matt. 24:15-16, 21-22).

Let us continue and read about this last week in Daniel 9:27: *"And he shall confirm the covenant with many for one week: and in the midst of the week he shall cause the sacrifice and the oblation to cease, and for the overspreading of abominations he shall make it desolate, even until the consummation, and that determined shall be poured upon the desolate."*

"Who is the "he" that is going to confirm the covenant with "many" in Israel for one week? What is this covenant that he is going to confirm? What is he going to do in the temple in the middle of the seventieth week? And what is it that is determined to be poured upon the desolate? We will discuss these questions in our next chapter.

There is only one possible antecedent of the pronoun "he," and that person is the prince described in the previous verse, the prince of the Roman Empire. The prince of the preceding verse was Titus. He was a prince of the Roman Empire, and the army of Rome under his authority did destroy Jerusalem and the temple. However, the Antichrist of verse twenty-seven will also be a prince of the Roman Empire. We must remember that the dispensation of grace is not in view here at all. The prophecy proceeds from the destruction of Jerusalem right into the tribulation period. Certainly, Titus made no treaty nor confirmed any covenant with the Jews. They used Josephus to intervene, and time and time again, Josephus tried to get the Jews to make a treaty with Titus, and they would not. It was their stubbornness to concede defeat that brought about their destruction. The reason they refused to agree to a peace treaty was that until the very last moment, they were expecting the Messiah to come and save them. The Messiah did not come because they did not cry out to God to send Jesus back. They rejected to the very end the truth that Jesus was the promised Savior.

As declared at the beginning of verse twenty-seven, the minute this prince of the Revived Roman Empire affixes his signature to a treaty with the government of Israel, the seventieth prophetic week will begin. The day this agreement is confirmed is the day the tribulation period will begin.

Notice in verse twenty-seven that this treaty that will be entered into between Israel and the Antichrist will not be just any ordinary run-of-the-mill treaty. It will be *the* covenant. Of course, we understand that God confirmed several covenants with Israel, but when the Scripture refers to "the covenant," there is only one covenant in consideration. It is the first covenant that God made with Abraham; an agreement entered into between Abraham and God that the land of Palestine would be given to the patriarch's seed for a future mighty nation, and an everlasting inheritance (Gen. 12:1-2). We also read about the covenant in Genesis 17:6-8: *"And I will make thee exceeding fruitful. . . . And I will establish my covenant between me and thee and thy seed after thee in their generations for an everlasting covenant. . . . And I will give unto thee, and to thy seed after thee, the land wherein thou art a stranger, all the land of Canaan, for an everlasting possession. . . ."*

Today we see the government of Israel trying desperately to get the Arab nations, the United Nations, or any representative coalition of nations, to recognize their right to the land of Palestine, the very same territory that Joshua conquered from the Canaanite tribes. The Arab nations that surround Israel and continually threaten their existence refuse to acknowledge that the Jews have any right at all to the land.

We read in Daniel 9:27 that in the middle of the week, which is the same as the middle of the tribulation, the Antichrist causes the sacrifice in the temple, and the evening worship service in the temple, to cease. He will command that it be halted. Of course, this will be a great shock to the Jews. It will be evidence that the Antichrist intends to break the terms of the covenant, and that he will no longer recognize Israel's right to the land.

We then read that "*. . . for the overspreading of abominations he shall make it desolate. . . .*" An abomination to Israel was the worship of false gods, the eating of things sacrificed to idols, or the polluting of the sanctuary with worship of other gods. There were other abominations, but the chiefest of all abominations was the contaminating of the faith of Israel with other religions and idol worship. Therefore, for the sake of the overspreading of the abomination of Antichrist, they claim that he is the only god, the temple worship services will be stopped, and the Antichrist will go into the temple and claim to be the Messiah, not only the Messiah of Israel, but the God of every nation. *"Let no man deceive you by any means: for that day shall not come, except there come a falling away first, and that man of sin be revealed, the son of perdition; Who opposeth and exalteth himself above all that is called God, or that is worshipped; so that he as God sitteth in the temple of God, shewing himself that he is God"* (2 Thess. 2:3-4). All the world by means of television will see the Antichrist sitting in the temple of Jerusalem, the temple that the Jews are going to build, showing himself as the Lord of all. He will claim to be Christ. This is the supreme abomination which Christ said would be the signal for Israel to flee from the land. *"When ye therefore shall see the abomination of desolation, spoken of by Daniel the prophet, stand in the holy place. . . . Then let them which be in Judaea flee into the mountains"* (Matt. 24:15-16).

The Antichrist himself will be the abomination of desolation — he will stand in the holy temple. His claiming to be the Messiah, the anointed One of God, will be the greatest abomination ever committed in the earth. But Satan has determined to put his own false christ upon the holy hill of Zion, and God will permit him to do it, but we are told in 2 Thessalonians 2:8: *"And then shall that Wicked be revealed, whom the Lord shall consume with the spirit of his mouth, and shall destroy with the brightness of his coming."*

Chapter Ten

We begin our study of chapter ten by reading the first four verses: *"In the third year of Cyrus king of Persia a thing was revealed unto Daniel, whose name was called Belteshazzar; and the thing was true, but the time appointed was long: and he understood the thing, and had understanding of the vision. In those days I Daniel was mourning three full weeks. I ate no pleasant bread, neither came flesh nor wine in my mouth, neither did I anoint myself at all, till three whole weeks were fulfilled. And in the four and twentieth day of the first month, as I was by the side of the great river, which is Hiddekel"* (Dan. 10:1-4).

At the time that Daniel received this, his last vision, he was at least ninety years of age (some commentaries state that he was ninety-three). We read in Daniel 1:21 that he continued in public service until the first year of Cyrus; therefore, it is evident that he had retired by the time this particular vision was received. Josephus wrote that because the Medes and the Persians held Daniel in such high regard, they built him a tower at Ecbatana in Media. It was in his own private castle on the bank of the Hiddekel River, also called the Tigris River, that Daniel spent the remaining years of his life. We are not informed how old he was when he died, because Daniel was the writer of the book and he could not record his own death. But he must have lived to be almost one hundred years old, and we read at the beginning of this chapter that though he was over ninety, his understanding was still good. And even though the vision itself was far away in space and time, Daniel still understood its importance to his country and the world.

The vision came to Daniel in a period of mourning. As far as phyical matters were concerned, the prophet had nothing to be sad or concerned about. The government had built him a mansion in the most beautiful spot in the kingdom, and he had everything furnished that the king's treasury could buy. However, at this time in the third year of Cyrus, Daniel was depressed and he went into a three-week period of mourning. We are not informed as to the reason for his doldrums, but we can be certain it was because things were not progressing in the return of the Jews as rapidly as Daniel thought they should be. When Daniel was sad and troubled, it was always over his nation. According to Ezra 1:1-4, it had now been two years since Cyrus signed the decree permitting Jews to return to their homeland, but only 49,697 had returned. Life for the Jews was much easier under the benevolent reign of both Darius and Cyrus. They had established homes, planted fields, established businesses, made friends, planted family roots; therefore, they were reticent to pull up stakes and go back to a land that most of them knew nothing about. The vast majority had been born in Babylon, and they felt no urgent need to rebuild Israel. Also, the land had been under the heel of oppressors for over seventy years. Jerusalem lay in ruins and the land was barren and desolate. Bands of robbers and savage tribes now roamed the mountains and valleys of Judah, and they did not look kindly upon the return of the Jews. They killed thousands of them when they did try to return. It is certainly understandable why the Jews did not want to return, and we read in the book of Esther about the majority of Israel who decided to remain behind in Persia.

However, when the Jews get too comfortable and too well situated in a foreign land, God has a way of stirring them up. We read of the Jew in Deuteronomy 32:9-12: *"For the Lord's portion is his people; Jacob is the lot of his inheritance. He found him in a desert land, and in the waste howling wilderness; he led him about, he instructed him, he kept him as the apple of his eye. As an eagle stirreth up her nest, fluttereth over her young, spreadeth abroad her wings, taketh them, beareth them on her wings: So the Lord alone did lead him, and there was no strange god with him."* Israel is God's chosen earthly people, and He has given them a particular land for their everlasting inheritance. When they become satisfied in a foreign nation, and begin to develop a national affinity for the nation in which they live, like an eagle, god stirs up their nest. When it becomes time for young eagles to get out of the nest and provide for themselves, the mother eagle will throw out the down, leaving only the rough sticks and sharp thorns. Then she will beat her wings over the young eagles to make them think she is going to beat them to death. She literally forces them out of their once comfortable nest. And as they flutter and fall down the rock cliffs, she catches them on her wings and bears them safely to a resting place.

Daniel's low emotional state during the third year of Cyrus was caused by the Jews not wanting to return to the land. He wanted God to stir them up. Some may wonder why Daniel himself did not go back, but he was doubtless very feeble and would have only been in the way. Israel needed fighters and builders, and the prophet was accomplishing more good for his country by staying behind and urging the younger Jews to go back.

We continue our study and read Daniel 10:5-6: *"Then I lifted up mine eyes, and looked, and behold a certain man clothed in linen, whose loins were girded with fine gold of Uphaz: His body also was like the beryl, and his face as the appearance of lightning, and his eyes as lamps of fire, and his arms and his feet like in colour to polished brass, and the voice of his words like the voice of a multitude."*

As Daniel was standing on the bank of the Tigris River which ran by his spacious estate, he looked up and above his head, suspended in the air, was a "certain" man. This man was dressed in linen clothes. His hips were as if they were made out of the fine gold of Uphaz. Uphaz was the place in Arabia where the finest and purest gold in the world was mined. The body of this man appeared as beryllium, which is similar in appearance to aluminum. The face of this man shone like lightning when it flashes on a dark night. The eyes were as a torch of fire, and his feet and arms were like polished brass in appearance. We might conclude that Daniel had a nightmare, except for the fact that other prophets and men of God have reported seeing a man very much like the one whom Daniel described. The various men who reported seeing such a person have used different descriptive language, but without doubt, all saw the same man. Instead of a white metal, they may have used snow, or a gold girdle intead of golden loins, or flames of fire instead of lamps of fire. For example we read John's description of a man he saw in a vision in Revelation 1:13-16: *"And in the midst of the seven candlesticks one like unto the Son of man, clothed with a garment down to the foot, and girt about the paps with a golden girdle. His head and his hairs were white like wool, as white as snow; and his eyes were as a flame of fire; And his feet like unto fine brass, as if they burned in a furnace; and his voice as the sound of many waters. And he had in his right hand seven stars: and out of his mouth went a sharp twoedged sword: and his countenance was as the sun shineth in his strength."*

If one were to give a description of the man Daniel saw to an artist, and gave the description of the man John saw to another artist, they would come up with similar drawings. The man whom John saw was the Lord Jesus Christ as He will appear when He returns to the earth.

There are reasons why we believe the "certain man" of Daniel chapter ten had to be Christ other than the similarity of His appearance to the Son of man whom John saw. In chapter nine, the prophet is informed about the Messiah who would be cut off at the end of the sixty-ninth prophetic week, yet nothing is said in chapter nine about this Messiah's restoration to Israel. The chapter closes with the seventieth week, but nothing is said about the Messiah coming back. Therefore, it appears evident that chapter ten begins with the conclusion of the seventieth week, and we know that Jesus will come again at the end of the tribulation. Daniel also said in verse one of chapter ten that the time appointed was long, meaning that this man whom he saw would have a relationship with Israel in the far distant future. The last reason we believe this "certain man" is Christ is that Daniel saw this vision on the twenty-fourth day of the first month, the week of Passover, and the Passover looked forward in type to the Passover Lamb who would be sacrificed for the sins of the world — the crucified Christ. We will discuss the "certain man's" confrontation with the prince of Persia when we get to verse fourteen.

We continue by reading Daniel 10:7-8: *"And I Daniel alone saw the vision: for the men that were with me saw not the vision; but a great quaking fell upon them, so that they fled to hide themselves. Therefore I was left alone, and saw this great vision, and there remained no strength in me: for my comeliness was turned in me into corruption, and I retained no strength."*

Another man besides Daniel and John came face-to-face with the glorified Christ, and this man was Saul of Tarsus. It is amazing how similar the effect was upon all three men. We read of Paul's experience in Acts 9:3-7: *"And as he journeyed, he came near Damascus: and suddenly there shined round about him a light from heaven: And he fell to the earth, and heard a voice saying unto him, Saul, Saul, why persecutest thou me? And he said, Who art thou, Lord? And the Lord said, I am Jesus whom thou persecutest: it is hard for thee to kick against the pricks. And he trembling and astonished said, Lord, what wilt thou have me to do? And the Lord said unto him, Arise, and go into the city, and it shall be told thee what thou must do. And the men which journeyed with him stood speechless, hearing a voice, but seeing no man."*

The men who were with Daniel were unsaved, and likewise the men with Saul. Even Saul himself was not saved at the time and he trembled and his eyes were blinded. Every unsaved person in the world will have to look upon Jesus Christ as He appeared to Daniel, John, and Paul. And like the unsaved with Daniel and Paul, they will tremble, quake with fear, and try to find a place to hide. We read in Revelation 6:14-17: *"And the heaven departed as a scroll when it is rolled together; and every mountain and island were moved out of their places. And the kings of the earth, and the great men, and the rich men, and the chief captains, and the mighty men, and every bondman, and every free man, hid themselves in the dens and in the rocks of the mountains; And said to the mountains and rocks, Fall on us, and hide us from the face of him that sitteth on the throne, and from the wrath of the Lamb: For the great day of his wrath is come; and who shall be able to stand?*

As we continue our study of chapter ten, we now read verses 9-11: "*Yet I heard the voice of his words: and when I heard the voice of his words, then was I in a deep sleep on my face, and my face toward the ground. And, behold, an hand touched me, which set me upon my knees and upon the palms of my hands. And he said unto me, O Daniel, a man greatly beloved, understand the words that I speak unto thee, and stand upright: for unto thee am I now sent. And when he had spoken this word unto me, I stood trembling.*"

We read in Matthew 17:2-8 that when Peter, James, and John saw the glorified Son of God they fell on their faces. Like Daniel, they could not help themselves. It is apparent from Scripture that when mortals stand before Christ in all His glory, they are impelled by their own mortal imperfection to fall down on their faces to the ground. We read in Philippians 2:8-11: "*. . . he humbled himself, and become obedient unto death, even the death of the cross. Wherefore God also hath highly exalted him,* *and given him a name which is above every name: That at the name of Jesus every knee should bow, of things in heaven, and things in earth, and things under the earth; And that every tongue should confess that Jesus Christ is Lord, to the glory of God the Father."*

We read in Matthew 17:7 that as Peter, James, and John were on their faces before the transfigured Jesus, He came and touched them and said: *". . . Arise, and be not afraid."* Jesus confronted them and removed their fear. And this is the message that Christ came to bring to all men. In John 6:20 we read that the disciples became greatly alarmed when they saw Jesus walking on the water, and he calmed them with the words: *". . . It is I; be not afraid."* In John 16:33, He said: *". . . be of good cheer; I have overcome the world."*

As Daniel was on his face, Christ came and touched the prophet gently on the shoulder, and said: *". . . fear not, O Daniel, a man greatly beloved."*

We notice that the touch of the Master's hand strengthened Daniel so that he was able to stand on his feet. We must remember Daniel had been fasting for three full weeks — twenty-one days. This would be exceedingly difficult for a young man, much less for a man of over ninety. Although Daniel was strengthened physically, he was still trembling in fear before the Great Person who appeared before him.

We continue and read Daniel 10:12-14: *"Then said he unto me, Fear not, Daniel: for from the first day that thou didst set thine heart to understand, and to chasten thyself before thy God, thy words were heard, and I am come for thy words. But the prince of the kingdom of Persia withstood me one and twenty days: but, lo, Michael, one of the chief princes, came to help me; and I remained there with the kings of Persia. Now I am come to make thee understand what shall befall thy people in the latter days: for yet the vision is for many days."*

Some believe that the "certain man" of Daniel chapter ten is an angel, and others believe that he is Gabriel. However, on previous occasions where Gabriel was sent to Daniel, he is named. Also, it is evident that Gabriel came by commandment, and the "certain man" of chapter ten came by his own volition. Also, neither an angel, Gabriel, or Michael are described as looking like the appearance of this man in chapter ten. The reason that some Bible expositors do not like to identify this man as Christ is that we read in verse thirteen that the prince of Persia prevented his coming to Daniel for twenty-one days, meaning from the very beginning of the prophet's prayers. It is disputed, with good reason, that this man could not possibly be Christ because the Lord would not have been delayed by this prince of Persia. He could have spoken one word and this being would have been rent asunder with the sword of His mouth. And they further contend that if we admit that an agent of Satan would resist Jesus Christ for twenty-one days, we ascribe too much power to the devil and not enough to God. We agree with this kind of reasoning up to a point, but we must keep in mind that

Jesus Christ could say a word or issue a command and every enemy of both God and man in the universe would be exterminated immediately. The Father has committed all power unto the Son, but this great glory and power was put aside so that He might take unto Himself the form of a man and die for sin. When Christ comes again He will come with power and great glory, but still every reference to the second coming declares that He will come as the Son of Man. He must reign as the Son of Man until He puts all enemies under His feet. Until this is accomplished, God has permitted the devil and his agents to inhabit sanctuaries in the heavens and deceive the world. It is evident that Christ appeared to Daniel as the Son of Man, His Kingdom Age nature, so that the prophet could see and talk with Him. It was in His form as the Son of Man that this evil power resisted Him, and even this was according to the permissive will of God. It is also evident that time was reversed, and we do not know what is involved in traveling through time and space. But just as Israel resisted Christ, this evil prince of Persia stood in His way. This evil power was not removed until Michael came to help.

Who is the prince of Persia? Certainly he was not Cyrus, because the "certain man" said he remained there with the kings of Persia, after Michael helped to put the prince of Persia on the run. To help us identify the prince of Persia, let us consider verse twenty-one. The Man told Daniel that Michael was his prince, meaning that Michael was the national guardian angel of Israel. Therefore, the prince of Persia would be an angelic being over the nation of Persia. Inasmuch as this creature resisted Christ, he would be an agent of Satan. In our next study, we will learn more about the demon powers that influence the world from high places. We read in Ephesians 6:11-12: *"Put on the whole armour of God, that ye may be able to stand against the wiles of the devil. For we wrestle not against flesh and blood, but against principalities, against powers, against the rulers of the darkness of this world, against spiritual wickedness in high places."* There are angelic beings who literally rule this world from high places. One of these beings was appointed by Satan to rule over Persia, and he was the one who withstood Christ.

We read in Revelation 12:7-9: *"And there was war in heaven: Michael and his angels fought against the dragon; and the dragon fought and his angels, And prevailed not; neither was their place found any more in heaven. And the great dragon was cast out, that old serpent, called the Devil, and Satan, which deceiveth the whole world: he was cast out into the earth, and his angels were cast out with him."* When Satan first rebelled against the authority of God, God could have destroyed him at that time. When man sinned against the commandment of God, God could have exterminated the human race. But God is preparing a family to inherit everlasting life and a perfect universe, and while this family is in the stage of preparation, or growing up as we might say, the Creator permits these revolutions in both the heavenly and earthly sphere. When Jesus Christ met the prince of Persia, He could have destroyed this evil person, but in the permissive will of God the nations are to be deceived until Christ comes to rule over them in power and great glory. But let us never forget that the universe is in the grip of a warfare — a war between God and the devil.

Josephus recorded evidence of spiritual warfare over Jerusalem just before it was destroyed. Peter promised Israel that if they would repent of their sins and cry out to God to send Jesus back, He would come back and deliver them from their enemies and bring in the kingdom. Had Israel repented of their sins and prayed to God to send back their Messiah, even up to the time of the destruction of the temple, Jesus would have returned. Even on the last days of the terrible Roman siege, the priests promised that Messiah would come. He did not come because they did not acknowledge the One whom they had crucified as the Redeemer. But we believe the prince of Israel, Michael, remained over Jerusalem with an army of angels, to come to Israel's aid should they call out to God to send Jesus back. In *The Wars of the Jews*, Josephus says:

> "*. . . A few days after the feast, on the one and twentieth day of the month of Jyar, a certain prodigious and incredible phenomenon appeared: I suppose the account of it would seem to be a fable, were it not related by those that saw it, and*

were not the events that followed it of so considerable a nature as to deserve such signals; for before sunsetting, chariots and troops of soldiers in their armour were seen running about among the clouds, and surrounding the cities. Moreover, at that feast which we call Pentecost, as the priests were going by night into the inner temple, as their custom was, to perform their sacred ministrations, they said that, in the first place, they felt a quaking, and heard a great noise, and after that they heard a sound as of a great multitude, saying, 'Let us remove hence.' But, what is still more terrible, there was one Jesus, the son of Ananus, a plebian and a husbandman, who, four years before the war began, to cry aloud, 'A voice from the east, a voice from the west, a voice from the four winds, a voice against Jerusalem and the holy house, a voice against the bridegrooms and the brides, and a voice against this whole people!"

In addition to the warfare in the heavens, Satan directs his warfare against man through unclean devils, unclean spirits, seducing spirits, and spirits of devils, or demons (Matt. 12:45; Luke 4:33; 1 Tim. 4:1; 1 Cor. 10:20-21). These are intelligent beings with power to hurt man physically and control him mentally and morally. These spirit beings can so take possession of a man or woman's body, that they will actually assume the personality of the evil spirit possessing them. In Ezekiel chapter twenty-eight it is indicated that the king of Tyre became so possessed of the devil that he became identified with the devil. Satan entered into Judas; and during the last half of the tribulation period, the Antichrist will become Satan incarnate. The Bible does not deny the power of demons and evil spirits over men; it warns men against them.

We continue and read Daniel 10:15-19: *"And when he had spoken such words unto me, I set my face toward the ground, and I became dumb. And, behold, one like the similitude of the sons of men touched my lips: then I opened my mouth, and spake, and said unto him that stood before me, O my lord, by the vision my sorrows are turned upon me, and I have retained no strength. For how can the servant of this my lord talk with this my lord? for as for me, straightway there remained no strength in me, neither is there breath left in me. Then there came again and touched me one like the appearance of a man, and he strengthened me, And said, O man greatly beloved, fear not: peace be unto thee, be strong, yea, be strong. And when he had spoken unto me, I was strengthened, and said, Let my lord speak; for thou hast strengthened me."*

After Daniel received the message which this one like the Son of Man came to give him, he was overwhelmed with grief. He sobbed: "O my lord, this vision you give me troubles me. My sorrows are turned upon me like a great and heavy stone. Such is the weight of this sorrow you place upon me; I have no strength to bear it." The prophecy which was given to Daniel was in greater detail than any previous revelation he received. From the first day that Daniel entered Babylon he prayed daily before His window for God to forgive the sins of Israel, restore Jerusalem and the temple, and bring in the everlasting kingdom of peace and righteousness. But now instead of peace, Daniel was made to understand that there would be wars and bloodshed over Jerusalem for hundreds of years before Messiah would bring peace. As Daniel considered the extent of this warfare over the holy land, it was more than he could bear. He saw his people continuing in unbelief and idolatry, and he saw foreign armies marching back and forth across his country, murdering, pillaging, and raping the women. And he looked up in the face of Jesus and said: "Lord, I can't bear it."

Daniel, when he saw what was coming upon his nation, hid his face. He saw the vile and treacherous Antiochus Epiphanes murder his people and desecrate the temple. He saw the bloody Roman siege of Jerusalem and the burning of the temple. He saw the Jews fleeing for their lives into all the world, and he saw them returning only to be persecuted at the hand of Antichrist, and he said: "Lord, let's just forget the whole thing. I would rather not talk to you about it. It is more than I can even bear to think about."

When the Lord touched Daniel again, the prophet received understanding as to why all these thing must come upon his people, and peace came to his soul. And so he turned to the Lord and said: "I feel much better now. Please continue and explain all these things which you have shown me." We read now the last two verses of the chapter: *"Then he said, Knowest thou wherefore I come unto thee? and now will I return to fight with the prince of Persia: and when I am gone forth, lo, the prince of Grecia will come. But I will shew thee that which is noted in the scripture of truth: and there is none that holdeth with me in these things, but Michael your prince"* (Dan. 10:20-21).

That the Lord was victorious over the prince of Persia, Satan's evil angel, is evident. The kings of Persia did deal kindly with Israel, and they allowed the Jews to return to rebuild Jerusalem and the temple. But even so, Satan would continue to stir up rulers and nations until the very end. But Daniel was assured that Michael, their prince, was ever ready to fight for Israel and to see that the plan and purpose of God for His earthly people would be fulfilled. Like Daniel, we sometimes want to turn our eyes from the world and forget all about these wars, rumours of wars, crime, and immorality. But through all the sorrows and trials, God assures us that His will will be done on earth even as it is in Heaven. We wait for the glorious appearing of our Lord Jesus Christ to bring in this kingdom from Heaven.

Chapter Eleven

We read in Daniel 11:1: *"Also I in the first year of Darius the Mede, even I, stood to confirm and to strengthen him."*

As we study the remainder of Daniel let us keep in mind that chapters ten, eleven, and twelve are all the account of one vision. As far as continuity is concerned, there should be no chapter separations. The speaker of Daniel 11:1 is not Daniel, but the "certain man" of chapter ten. The setting does not revert back to the first year of Darius the Mede, but rather dates back to an event which happened in the first year of Darius. It is difficult to ascertain just what this event was, because it is unclear to whom the personal pronoun "him" in verse one refers. It could refer back to Darius, Michael, the prince of Grecia, the prince of Persia, or Daniel.

We read in the sixth chapter of Daniel that the Lord shut the mouths of the lions and that Daniel prospered in the reign of Darius. It was also in the first year of Darius that Daniel received the vision of the seventy prophetic weeks. There is no specific scripture relating to the strengthening of Darius by the Lord; therefore, evidence would indicate that Daniel rather than Darius is the principal subject of Daniel 11:1.

Beginning with verse two of chapter eleven, to the

end of the chapter, we have the prophetic record of every important Gentile ruler in the world from the time of Cyrus to the appearance of Antichrist. Of course, we must understand that the dispensation of grace is not in view here, and important world figures during the dispensation of grace are not mentioned. But this still does not reduce the importance of this prophecy, because we are shown here step-by-step the rise and fall of rulers during the four hundred ninety year period that God would deal with Israel. At the end of the four hundred ninety year period the last ruler would appear, and he would be the Antichrist. Without a doubt, this is the most remarkable prophecy in all the Bible, and it is no wonder that it was revealed personally by the Lord Jesus Christ. We read in Luke 21:19 that Jesus is the master prophet, and the testimony of Jesus is the spirit of prophecy.

We now continue with Daniel 11:2: *"And now will I shew thee the truth. Behold, there shall stand up yet three kings in Persia; and the fourth shall be far richer than they all: and by his strength through his riches he shall stir up all against the realm of Grecia."*

At the time this revelation was given to Daniel it was prophecy, but as we read it today, we find it to be history. The three principal Persian kings who sat upon the throne after Cyrus were Ahasuerus (Ezra 4:6; Est. 1:1), Artaxerxes, and Darius Hystaspis. Cyrus died in 529 B.C., and these three kings ruled over the empire between 529 B.C. and 485 B.C. The king after Darius was Xerxes. The kingdom had prospered under the four former kings, and Xerxes inherited a bulging treasury. He used the surplus to equip an army of two million men to conquer Europe. He launched his military campaign across the straits of Thermopylae into Greece. His army corp of engineers placed ships side by side across the straits and the huge Persian army marched into Greece dry shod. This Persian military innovation is still used by modern armies to transport troops and armored units across rivers. Seven days and nights were required for the passing of this army of two million men across the Hellespont. In spite of the overwhelming superiority in numbers of the Persian army, the smaller but better trained Grecian army put up a stout defense and a horrible slaughter ensued. And even though the Greeks were driven back and Xerxes did manage to advance into Greece, he never completely conquered the nation and the Grecians began looking forward to a time of revenge. Meanwhile, the committing of the bulk of Persian manpower to the war effort and the draining of the treasury for weapons of war so weakened the Persian Empire that after Xerxes, no king of any great importance arose. Therefore, according to the prophecy, the fourth king after Cyrus used great riches to stir up the entire realm against Greece, but in so doing, he bankrupted the nation and it began to decline in power.

We continue and read Daniel 11:3-4: *"And a mighty king shall stand up, that shall rule with great dominion, and do according to his will. And when he shall stand up, his kingdom shall be broken, and shall be divided toward the four winds of heaven; and not to his posterity, nor according to his dominion which he ruled: for his kingdom shall be plucked up, even for others beside those."*

This part of the prophecy concerns the fall of the Persian Empire to Alexander of Greece. As we have already discussed in studying the other prophecies in Daniel that refer to Greece, Alexander died of swamp fever in Babylon and his great empire was broken into four parts. A division was given to each of his four generals: Cassander took Macedonia; Lysimachus took Thrace; Seleucus took Syria; and, Ptolemy took Egypt. And as the prophecy indicates, there was continual strife and turmoil within these four divisions until they were absorbed under one authority in the Roman Empire.

Some students of the Scriptures believe the scene passes from the breakup of the Grecian Empire on into the time of the end. There are certain similarities between the wars and conflicts described between verses five and thirty-six to wars of the past three decades between Israel and the Arab nations. However, the involvement of women in these wars would seem to indicate that the prophecies between verses five and thirty-six relate to the struggles between the four divisions of the Grecian Empire, and particularly the wars between Syria and Egypt.

We continue and read Daniel 11:5: *"And the king of the south shall be strong, and one of his princes;*

and he shall be strong above him, and have dominion;
his dominion shall be a great dominion."

The prophecy at this point narrows in scope to describe the wars between the king of the south and the king of the north to Syria. Daniel was made to understand that after the fall of the Persian Empire, his nation would become a buffer state between these two powers. Therefore, his people would suffer greatly because Israel would be a battleground continually for several hundred years. This was one reason why Daniel did not want to hear the conclusion of the prophecy.

Concerning verse five, the king of the south was Ptolemy Soter who ruled Egypt well and made of it a strong nation. At the time the kingdom was divided, Seleucus Nicator was made vice-regent of Babylonia, but a man by the name of Antigonus conspired to take over the province and Nicator had to flee to Egypt. In Egypt Nicator was received by his old friend Ptolemy and was made a prince of his empire. Ptolemy financed a military expedition for Seleucus Nicator, and he regained his position of authority in Babylon. From that starting point, he enlarged his province until it extended from India and included Syria and Assyria. Therefore, his dominion became a greater dominion than Egypt.

Next we read Daniel 11:6: *"And in the end of years they shall join themselves together; for the king's daughter of the south shall come to the king of the north to make an agreement: but she shall not retain the power of the arm; neither shall he stand, nor his arm: but she shall be given up, and they that brought her, and he that begat her, and he that strengthened her in these times."*

This verse describes the political intrigue that arose when it was decided that it would be to the advantage of both Syria and Egypt to join the two countries together in a mutual aid treaty. The daughter of the king of the south, Bernice, was given by Ptolemy II of Egypt, to Antiochus Theos of Syria, called the Divine. Ptolemy sent along a handsome dowry with his daughter. The demand made by Ptolemy upon Antiochus of Syria was that he must divorce his wife, Laodice, and declare his two children by her as illegitimate offspring of another man. Ptolemy planned to place his own heir upon the throne of Syria, and possibly bring about the unification of the two countries into one nation.

But soon after Bernice married Antiochus Theos, her father, Ptolemy II died. Antiochus then demoted her to the status of a concubine and brought back Laodice as his queen. But Laodice, playing the part of a jealous and spurned woman, murdered both Antiochus and Bernice. Therefore, as the prophecy indicated, Bernice was given up and the entire plot ended in disaster for all concerned. Upon hearing that Bernice had been murdered, her brother Euergetes set out to avenge his sister's death. He plundered Syria, burned their temples, and brought back to Egypt much gold, silver, and idols. Jerusalem served as a way station for the Egyptian army, and much suffering and hardships were brought upon the Jews. The exploits of Ptolemy Euergetes in revenge for the murders of his sister in Syria were prophesied in Daniel 11:7-9: *"But out of a branch of her roots shall one stand up in his estate, which shall come with an army, and shall enter into the fortress of the king of the north, and shall deal against them, and shall prevail: And shall also carry captives into Egypt their gods, with their princes, and with their precious vessels of silver and of gold; and he shall continue more years than the king of the north. So the king of the south shall come into his kingdom, and shall return into his own land."*

Jerome wrote that Euergetes brought back from Syria forty thousand talents of silver, four thousand talents of gold, and two thousand costly idol statues. But this Egyptian campaign only served to perpetuate the bitterness that existed between Syria and Egypt, and Israel continued to serve as a pawn, and a battleground between the two powers. All this was revealed to Daniel and it proves the divine inspiration of our Holy Bible. And through all these wars, famines, and tribulations, the Lord assured Daniel that His plan and purpose would prevail.

We continue our study by reading Daniel 11:10: *"But his sons shall be stirred up, and shall assemble a multitude of great forces: and one shall certainly come, and overflow, and pass through: then shall he return, and be stirred up, even to his fortress."*

After the sacking of Syria by Egypt, the sons of Antiochus Theos and the sons of former Syrian rulers put aside their differences to raise a large army to avenge their honor and recapture the national wealth. After an assassination and much power grabbing, the command ended up in the hands of another Syrian Antiochus, and by this time, another Ptolemy was on the throne in Egypt — Ptolemy Philopater. As indicated in the prophecy, Antiochus marched southward through Jerusalem with his huge army, and the Jews and their holy city were again trodden underfoot by the Gentiles. The city was robbed of all food and provisions, the men were killed in the streets, and the women were raped. After passing through Palestine, the Syrian army attacked the Egyptian fortress in Gaza, the strongpoint that guarded the eastern approach. This was in the year 218 B.C., and this event brings us to the end of verse ten.

Reading next Daniel 11:11-12: *"And the king of the south shall be moved with choler, and shall come forth and fight with him, even with the king of the north: and he shall set forth a great multitude; but the multitude shall be given into his hand. And when he hath taken away the multitude, his heart shall be lifted up; and he shall cast down many ten thousands: but he shall not be strengthened by it."*

History records that the Egyptian fortress at Gaza delayed the Syrian army long enough for Philopater to marshal his entire army. The two forces met at Raphia near Gaza. The surprise effect which the Syrian hoped for was gone, and the Egyptian army, being fresher and better supplied, soundly defeated the invaders. Philopater, being somewhat of a playboy, was delighted with the victory because it seemed to prove to the masses that he could also be a general of the army. But also being enraged at the Syrians, he ordered many captives to be slaughtered. And tens of thousands were cast down as the prophecy states — they were killed without mercy. Had Philopater decided to march on Syria, all the land from Damascus to India would have been his for lustful pursuits; and so in order to bring peace, he made an agreement with Antiochus, and the Syrian king took what remained of his army and marched back to his own country.

Josephus records that Philopater's father, the brother of Bernice, was a godly man. He did not honor the gods of Egypt, but rather came to Jerusalem to offer up a sacrifice to the God of Israel. Philopater, although not an honorable man, inherited a friendship toward the Jews from his father. The entire business affairs of Egypt were entrusted to the Jews and thousands moved from Israel to Alexandria to become merchants. After the death of Philopater, also called Philometer, the new king decided to kill the Jews. Josephus writes that all the Jews in Alexandria were gathered together in the town square and stripped naked. Elephants belonging to the Egyptian army were first made drunk, and then turned loose on the helpless and naked Jews. But instead of charging and trampling the Jews, the elephants turned on their handlers and the soldiers guarding them and many were killed. The Jews were subsequently spared.

We continue and read Daniel 11:13: *"For the king of the north shall return, and shall set forth a multitude greater than the former, and shall certainly come after certain years with a great army and with much riches."*

The importance of this verse is to expose the folly of Philopater in making a peace treaty with Antiochus of Syria. The Syrian ruler began immediately to rebuild his army to start a new invasion of Egypt.

We go to Daniel 11:14: *"And in those times there shall many stand up against the king of the south: also the robbers of thy people shall exalt themselves to establish the vision; but they shall fall."* This verse indicates a time of turmoil and rebellion in Egypt, and it contains a reference to the persecution of the Jews in Alexandria which we have already mentioned. The revolt in Egypt failed, the Jews were saved, and an infant king was instituted as the new royal monarch. It was also at this time that the Romans began to move westward and a mutual aid treaty was signed between Rome and Egypt.

This brings us to verse fifteen. Let us continue with Daniel 11:15-19: *"So the king of the north shall come, and cast up a mount, and take the most fenced cities: and the arms of the south shall not withstand, neither his chosen people, neither shall there be any strength to withstand. But he that cometh against him shall do according to his own will, and none shall stand before him: and he shall stand in the glorious land, which by his hand shall be consumed. He shall also set his face to enter with the strength of his whole kingdom, and upright ones with him; thus shall he do: and he shall give him the daughter of women, corrupting her: but she shall not stand on his side, neither be for him. After this shall he turn his face unto the isles, and shall take many: but a prince for his own behalf shall cause the reproach offered by him to cease; without his own reproach he shall cause it to turn upon him. Then he shall turn his face toward the fort of his own land: but he shall stumble and fall, and not be found."*

In order to reach Egypt, Antiochus the Great had to first conquer Israel, which was at that time under the protection of Egypt and guarded by an Egyptian army. Antiochus was successful in overrunning the Egyptian garrison stationed in Israel, and in Israel he was able to do according to his will because the Jews, relying upon the protection of Egypt, had no army to resist him.

As Antiochus regrouped his forces for a march on Egypt, some rather disturbing news came to his attention. The Egyptians had signed a mutual aid pact with the Romans, a powerful new nation rising up in the west. Therefore, he changed his plans. The monarch of Egypt at that time was a young boy, seven years old. His name was Ptolemy Epiphanes. Antiochus had a young daughter about the same age, so he left his army behind and traveled on to Egypt as an ambassador of good will, taking his daughter with him. The name of his daughter was Cleopatra. He proposed the royal household of Egypt and the royal household of Syria be united in peace by arranging a marriage between Cleopatra and Epiphanes. Now here is a remarkable fulfillment of prophecy. We are told that the king of the north, Antiochus, would corrupt the young girl that he would give to the king of the south for political reasons. As soon as the marriage was consummated, Cleopatra was supposed to gain control of Egypt and turn the nation over to her greedy father. Therefore, Cleopatra was exposed to deceit and intrigue at a very early age. She got the idea from her father that the purpose of sex was for women to use to get all they could from men. The marriage between Cleopatra and Epiphanes was brought about when both were twelve years of age — five years after Antiochus brought her to Egypt.

Cleopatra learned her lesson well, and she began her career of deceit and trickery by betraying her own father. She exposed his plan to her young husband, and in turn he encouraged the Romans to attack Syrian shipping. Cleopatra herself sent congratulations to the Romans for their victories over her father.

All this political mystery, intrigue, and bitterness is embedded deep within the history of the Middle East, and time has not washed away these ugly memories. This is another reason why there can be no peace in the Middle East between Israel and the Arabs until Christ returns. As far as Cleopatra's father is concerned, he finally was goaded into defending his ships against the Roman navy. He fitted out three hundred warships to fight the ships of Rome and plunder their ports. This was the fulfillment of the prophecy that he would turn his face toward the isles and take many. However, his venture soon ended in disaster. A young naval commander of Rome, a member of Caesar's household by the name of Scipio Asiasticus, led a fleet of Roman warships against him, and the bulk of his Mediterranean naval force was sunk. This fulfilled the prophecy that a prince would end his reproach. After Antiochus returned to Antioch, he sent an ambassador to the Romans to effect a peace arrangement. The peace terms laid down by the Romans were harsh. He had to relinquish all his holdings in Europe and much of Western Turkey. He also had to pay twenty-three hundred thirty talents to Rome at the signing of the peace treaty, and one thousand talents a year for the next twelve years. A few months later, when robbing the temples in his own provinces for money to pay the war obligation, he was killed in the temple of Bel in Elymais. Therefore, the consummation of the prophecy concerning Antiochus that he would stumble and fall in his own land was fulfilled in every detail!

All these things about Antiochus and Cleopatra were prophesied in Daniel over three hundred years before they happened. The downfall of Antiochus was brought about by his own daughter.

We continue and read Daniel 11:20: *"Then shall*

stand up in his estate a raiser of taxes in the glory of the kingdom: but within a few days he shall be destroyed, neither in anger, nor in battle." Antiochus, the father of Cleopatra, also called Antiochus the Great, was succeeded upon the throne of Syria by his oldest son, Seleucus Philopater. The new ruler of Syria inherited the heavy war debt imposed upon his father by the Romans. In order to meet the yearly assessment of one thousand talents, he placed a heavy tax upon all the Jews in Israel. Philopater had been on the throne for twelve years, and being extremely pressed to meet the last payment to Rome, sent his treasurer to Jerusalem to confiscate the gold and silver vessels in the temple. However, within a few days, as the prophecy states, he was poisoned. It is not known who poisoned him. We can only guess that it may have been by a Jew in order to save the holy vessels. In any event, though the Jews were forced to help pay off the war debt of Syria, the temple was spared for a time. We again see how Israel suffered under the reign of the Syrian ruler, Seleucus Philopater.

We next read Daniel 11:21-31: *"And in his estate shall stand up a vile person, to whom they shall not give the honour of the kingdom: but he shall come in peaceably, and obtain the kingdom by flatteries. And with the arms of a flood shall they be overflown from before him, and shall be broken; yea, also the prince of the covenant. And after the league made with him he shall work deceitfully: for he shall come up, and shall become strong with a small people. He shall enter peaceably even upon the fattest places of the province; and he shall do that which his fathers have not done, nor his fathers' fathers; he shall scatter among them the prey, and spoil, and riches: yea, and he shall forecast his devices against the strong holds, even for a time. And he shall stir up his power and his courage against the king of the south with a great army; and the king of the south shall be stirred up to battle with a very great and mighty army; but he shall not stand: for they shall forecast devices against him. Yea, they that feed of the portion of his meat shall destroy him, and his army shall overflow: and many shall fall down slain. And both these kings' hearts shall be to do mischief, and they shall speak lies at one table; but it shall not prosper: for yet the end shall be at the time appointed. Then shall he return into his land with great riches; and his heart shall be against the holy covenant; and he shall do exploits, and return to his own land. At the time appointed he shall return, and come toward the south; but it shall not be as the former, or as the latter. For the ships of Chittim shall come against him: therefore he shall be grieved, and return, and have indignation against the holy covenant: so shall he do; he shall even return, and have intelligence with them that forsake the holy covenant. And arms shall stand on his part, and they shall pollute the sanctuary of strength, and shall take away the daily sacrifice, and they shall place the abomination that maketh desolate."*

This particular portion of the prophecy given to

Daniel concerning those things that would come upon the Jews, pertains to the reign of a Syrian ruler who followed Seleucus Philopater. This man was Philopater's young brother, who became known as Antiochus Epiphanes. He was also the brother of Cleopatra, and it would appear that he was born after Cleopatra had been betrothed to Ptolemy Epiphanes of Egypt. We believe that he must have been named after Cleopatra's first husband. History records that Antiochus Epiphanes was every bit as deceitful, treacherous, and cunning as his sister. He is spoken of in the text as a "vile person." We will not try to show in great detail how all these prophecies in verses twenty-one through thirty-one were fulfilled in Antiochus Epiphanes. Those who are interested in proving the prophecy point by point can obtain a copy of *The History of the Jews* by Josephus and compare the record of this man to the prophetic account in Daniel.

We are informed in verse twenty-one that he would come into his kingdom by flattery. Like his sister, he was a great manipulator and a good talker. Antiochus Epiphanes was not the rightful heir to the throne. His nephew, Demetrius, was the next in line. However, he used his cunning ways and glib tongue to convince the royal family that he was the rightful heir. He brought about the downfall of the Jewish High Priest Onias III, called in verse twenty-two the prince of the covenant. The true prince is the Lord Jesus Christ, but the wording here is so given as to refer to both Antiochus Epiphanes and the Antichrist. It will be Antichrist who will commit the ultimate abomination of desolation. But the Antichrist will be much like Antiochus Epiphanes, and what this ancient Syrian ruler did during his reign paralleled much of what the Antichrist will do. And, as we have already pointed out, there is scriptural evidence that the Antichrist will be a descendant of Antiochus. But we will make the initial application to the historical period of 175 B.C. to 164 B.C. Antiochus Epiphanes was a polished liar. He made arrangements and kept them only as long as it was to his advantage. When he dealt with the Romans, in order not to arouse their opposition, he pretended to have only a small army, but then he suddenly attacked Egypt with a huge army. As far as Antiochus is concerned, this could be the fulfillment of the prophecy that he would become strong with a small people.

Through deceit and treachery, he was able to overcome the army of Egypt and capture Ptolemy Philometer. He used Philometer to try to gain control of all Egypt, but they worked so deceitfully against each other that neither one could believe what the other was saying. In verse twenty-four we note that this ruler would scatter his spoils and do what neither his fathers nor his fathers' fathers would do. His own father was saddled with the huge Roman debt and had to plunder to satisfy the Romans. With the debt being paid off, Antiochus Epiphanes bought loyalty by dividing the spoils among his close friends and army officers. On his way back through Israel from Egypt, he killed forty thousand Jews and robbed the temple of eighteen hundred talents. His army raped the women and he hanged all the young Jewish males who were circumcised. There were too many other terrible things that he did to the Jewish people to mention. We can certainly understand why Daniel wept when he was shown what was to come upon his people.

We read in verse thirty that the ships of Chittim would come against this king and force him to retreat from the south. The fulfillment of this prophecy came when Antiochus made a second expedition against Egypt. His first campaign objective was to take Alexandria. But when his army arrived at Alexandria, a Roman fleet lay anchored in the bay. The fleet commander met Antiochus and informed him that by a decree from the Roman senate, he must leave Egypt alone and return to his own country or he would be opposed by the Roman army and navy. To gain time, Antiochus told the Roman commander that he would have to consult with his advisers first. But knowing the deceitful ways of the Syrian, Popilius, the naval officer, promptly drew a circle around him and said: "Before you step out of that circle give such an answer as I may report to the senate." Antiochus, seeing that his hand was called, agreed to leave.

Being deprived of Egypt, Antiochus withdrew to Jerusalem and vented his fury a second time on the defenseless Jews. His treatment of the Jews could be compared to kicking his dog because he lost a fight. He paid money to some of the ungodly Jews to spy on their own people, and anyone who said anything against him was hung in public as a warning to others. Josephus reported the ultimate abomination which Antiochus committed in Israel. Quoting the historian:

"And when the king had built an idol altar upon God's altar, he slew swine upon it, and so offered a sacrifice neither according to the law, nor the Jewish religious worship. . . ."

We understand by Josephus that Antiochus first tore out the altar of God, and built an idol altar in its place. It was upon this idol altar that the swine was offered. This idol altar was actually an image of their false god, with a place to burn their sacrifice at the bottom. This was representative of what the Antichrist will do when he stops the daily sacrifice in the temple during the tribulation and places his own image in the temple.

In verse thirty-one we notice that this deed is referred to as the "abomination that maketh desolate." The abomination of desolation is mentioned specifically four times in the Bible. In Daniel 9:27 it is stated explicitly that it will occur in the middle of the tribulation. Here in Daniel 11:31 it is indicated that it was committed by Antiochus Epiphanes, but this deed was only representative of the greater abomination and the great desolation in Israel that will come with Antichrist standing in the temple. In Daniel 12:11 the abomination of desolation is again placed in the middle of the tribulation, and it is also placed in the tribulation by Jesus in Matthew 24:15, 21: *"When ye therefore shall see the abomination of desolation, spoken of by Daniel the prophet, stand in the holy place, (whoso readeth, let him understand:) . . . For then shall be great tribulation, such as was not since the beginning of the world to this time, no, nor ever shall be."*

As we noted in our study of other prophecies relating to Antiochus, his hold on Israel was broken by the revolt of fearless Jews under the leadership of the Maccabees. Antiochus Epiphanes died in Syria of malnutrition. His loss of Israel so disturbed him that he could not eat and he died. With the victory over his Jerusalem army by the Jews, he realized that he could never become a ruler of all the world. His vision of a world empire crumbled, and like his sister Cleopatra, he died in his own disillusionment and misery.

We continue and read Daniel 11:32-35: *"And such as do wickedly against the covenant shall he corrupt by flatteries: but the people that do know their God shall be strong, and do exploits. And they that understand among the people shall instruct many: yet they shall fall by the sword, and by flame, by captivity, and by spoil, many days. Now when they shall fall, they shall be holpen with a little help: but many shall cleave to them with flatteries. And some of them of understanding shall fall, to try them, and to purge, and to make them white, even to the time of the end: because it is yet for a time appointed."*

Daniel is informed that even from the time of Antiochus Epiphanes to the time of the end, a period of many days, the Jews would be taken captive and made slaves, their property would be the spoils of plunder, and many would fall by the sword. Others would be deceived and used deceitfully, and they would be as a plague upon the face of the earth, until the very end of the age. This has happened just as the prophecy given to Daniel declares.

In verses thirty-three through thirty-five, it is declared that from the time of Antiochus Epiphanes and the appearance of the ships of Chittim, the Roman navy, in the Mediterranean to the time of the end, the Jews would go into captivity and fall by the sword. We know that this happened during the dispensation of grace, and the prophecy here in Daniel corresponds to our Lord's prophecy concerning Israel in Luke 21:24: *"And they shall fall by the edge of the sword, and shall be led away captive into all nations: and Jerusalem shall be trodden down of the Gentiles, until the times of the Gentiles be fulfilled."*

Now from verse thirty-five where it says "the time of the end," the prophecy skips all the way over the dispensation of grace to the seventieth week of Daniel. And from our own pivotal point in time, the eleventh chapter of Daniel changes from history to prophecy. Therefore we move into the future as we read verse thirty-six: *"And the king shall do according to his will; and he shall exalt himself, and magnify himself above every god, and shall speak marvellous things against*

*the God of gods, and shall prosper till the indignation
be accomplished: for that that is determined shall be
done."*

Thus far in our study of Daniel we have brought
out so many things about the Antichrist, his nature,
and his empire that it is difficult to say anything else
about him without being repetitious. Nevertheless, let
us glean additional truths about this coming world
ruler from verse thirty-six as the Spirit reveals them to
our understanding.

1. We read first that the king shall do according to his
   will. This king, as stated in preceding verses, is the
   king of the north. He is the ruler of a ten-nation
   federation, and because he is the prince of the
   Roman Empire (Dan. 9:26-27), we believe he will be
   the president of the Common Market of Europe,
   which will ultimately become the Revived Roman
   Empire. We read of the ten kings over the ten
   nations of his empire in Revelation 17:13: *"These
   have one mind, and shall give their power and
   strength unto the beast."* Therefore, this ruler over
   this powerful kingdom will do according to his will.
   He will tolerate no opposition in the entire world.
   According to Revelation 13:11-18, every person
   must take his mark and worship him or be killed.
2. We notice next that this willful king will exalt
   himself above every god. There are several move-
   ments afoot today to bring all religions under one
   roof. The World Council of Churches is working to

build a one-world church. The fact that the willful king of Daniel 11:36 will also be the Antichrist is proved by Revelation 13:15 where it is declared that all the world will worship him and he will exalt himself above every god.

3. We read also that the willful king will prosper. This dictator's kingdom will prosper and he will enlarge his dominion and he will overcome all opposition until the indignation is accomplished. This will be the abomination that maketh desolate — his standing in the temple of God in Jerusalem showing himself to all the world as the God of gods. The Jews will flee from the land and Palestine will become a barren desolation. It will not rain for three and a half years, and the Middle East will become a wasteland. We read that this is determined and God will permit it to happen. The devil's man will have his day. He will have his day because the people of the world will become so sinful and wicked that they will want a wicked man to rule over them. When Israel cried for a king, God told Samuel to anoint them a dictator. The world is turning their backs on Christ today and crying for an Antichrist, and God will allow the nations to have their Antichrist for a season.

We continue and read more about the willful king in Daniel 11:37: *"Neither shall he regard the God of his fathers, nor the desire of women, nor regard any god: for he shall magnify himelf above all."*

There are many Bible scholars who contend that the Antichrist will be a Jew because of the statement that he will not regard the God of his fathers, meaning father Abraham, father Isaac, and father Jacob. Also, it is brought out that in order for the Jews to accept the Antichrist as Messiah and accept his confirmation of the covenant, he would have to be one of their own people who had credentials indicating that he was of the lineage of David. We have also discussed the possibility that the Antichrist will be Judas, whom Satan will bring up from the bottomless pit. Judas and the Antichrist are the only two men mentioned in the Bible by the specific title "Son of Perdition." We are also informed that when Judas committed suicide, he went to his own place — something said of no other person. According to the one hundred ninth psalm, the posterity of Judas would be cut off. Therefore, the Antichrist could not come of Judas' lineage except that he come back as the traitor himself. According to Revelation 17:8, the Antichrist will ascend up out of the bottomless pit; therefore, it is within the realm of scriptural possibility that the beast and Judas could be one and the same. However, there is some area of doubt created because Daniel chapter eleven deals specifically with rulers of foreign nations who will overrun Israel and tread down Jerusalem until Christ returns. Also, Revelation chapter thirteen is given in Gentile terminology, and it is in Revelation that the Antichrist is presented as both a political dictator and a false god. It is possible that the Antichrist will be half

Jewish and half Syrian, and yet become president of the Common Market nations. We will certainly admit that this is the most unusual racial mixture the world could produce; however, the Antichrist will have to be a most unusual man to bring about even a temporary ceasefire in the Middle East and get the Arab nations to recognize Israel's right to Palestine. Someone who is half-Jewish and half-Arab might be able to do it. Regardless, whether he be Jew, Arab, or Grecian, or all three, he will not regard the God of his fathers, because we are plainly informed that he will not regard the God of his fathers or any god; he will magnify himself above all gods.

We continue with Daniel 11:38: *"But in his estate shall he honour the God of forces: and a god whom his fathers knew not shall he honour with gold, and silver, and with precious stones, and pleasant things."*

The words "in his estate" mean "in his place." This means that in the place of the God of his people, he will pay honour to another god. This strange god is called the god of forces.

Before we continue on to the next verse, let us touch on another point that we overlooked in verse thirty-seven. We are informed that this willful king, the Antichrist, will not regard the desire of women. Of course, we know that the desire of all women in Israel was to have a son in order that they might be the vessel God would use to perpetuate the bloodline through which the Messiah would come. Israel, even today, does not acknowledge that the Messiah has come. The

Jews are still expecting some woman in Israel to give birth to the Savior. His not regarding this desire could explain our Lord's warning to the women of Israel during the tribulation in Matthew 24:19: *"And woe unto them that are with child, and to them that give suck in those days!"* The Antichrist may attempt to kill all babies and pregnant women in Israel. However, there is another possible explanation of this scripture. We are told in several prophecies that in the last days there would be a great increase in homosexuality. Jesus said that it would be as it was at Sodom. We are seeing this alarming rise in sexual perversion to the extent that marriages between members of the same sex are becoming quite common. The laws against homosexuality have been removed in almost every country in the world. By the time Antichrist appears, homosexuals may be considered to be more normal than heterosexuals. Therefore, the prophecy that the Antichrist will not regard the desire of woman could simply mean that he will be a sexual pervert. Or it may have a double meaning: he will kill the babies and pregnant women in Israel and also be a homosexual. Certainly, we are living in those days in which these prophecies concerning the Antichrist are coming into view. We can already see his shadow; therefore, can the beast be far behind?

We continue in our study and read Daniel 11:39: *"Thus shall he do in the most strong holds with a strange god, whom he shall acknowledge and increase with glory: and he shall cause them to rule over many, and shall divide the land for gain."*

What we actually have in verses thirty-seven through thirty-nine is a picture of the Antichrist subsidizing the one-world religious system. He will heap upon it much gold, silver, and precious stones. This corresponds to the picture we have in Revelation chapter seventeen of the harlot woman riding on the back of the beast adorned with gold and all kinds of costly array. We are also informed in verse thirty-nine that the Antichrist will glorify the false prophet in the greatest stronghold of the world. Where are the greatest strongholds of the world today? They are located in Washington, D.C., Moscow, Peking, Paris, Berlin, Cairo, and Jerusalem. In other words, the Antichrist and the false prophet will make personal appearances in the major capitals of the world. Even today, such a trip would not require over a week at most. It has also become quite popular for important political and religious figures to make world tours. During the tribulation period, the titular head of world politics and the head of the world church will get together and make a tour of the major cities of the world. People will turn out by the millions to greet them.

Note in verse thirty-nine that the Antichrist will cause them to rule over many. It is according to the plan of our Lord to have the saints rule over the earth. We read in Revelation 20:4: *"And I saw thrones, and they sat upon them, and judgment was given unto them: and I saw the souls of them that were beheaded for the witness of Jesus, and for the word of God, and which had not worshipped the beast, neither his image, neither had received his mark upon their foreheads, or in their hands; and they lived and reigned with Christ a thousand years."*

The Antichrist will attempt to prevent the saints from ruling over the earth by appointing his own political admirers and followers as rulers over the earth. He will also divide the land of Palestine into provinces and appoint his own men over Israel. Jesus promised the apostles that they would sit upon twelve thrones judging the twelve tribes of Israel; therefore, the Antichrist may divide Israel into twelve divisions and appoint a governor over each one. In Revelation 11:8-13, we read that when the Antichrist kills the two witnesses, that all the important people in the government of his empire will gather in Jerusalem for a big celebration, and seven thousand of them will be killed in a great earthquake.

These four verses evidently describe the mounting troubles of Antichrist at the end of his reign and just before Christ returns. From other scriptures, we know that the kings who rule over his ten-nation empire will stay with him all the way. However, as he moves into the Middle East, taking control of Israel and most countries surrounding Israel, there will be growing unrest in the other powerful nations. We read here that the king of the south, Egypt, and another king of the north, will combine forces to drive him from Israel.

In verse forty-two the Word informs us that Egypt will not escape the hand of Antichrist. We do not know exactly what this means, but it is evident that a great judgment will come upon Egypt in the end of the age. In Ezekiel 29:11-13, it is prophesied that in the last days a judgment will be visited upon Egypt and the land would be desolate and polluted for forty years. If even a dog walks over the land it will die. This has never happened to this day, and it would appear that it will occur when the Antichrist puts his hand upon Egypt. This judgment will probably be in the form of nuclear contamination from atomic bombs. We are also informed that Ethiopia and Libya will be at his steps.

Political, military, and economic conditions in the Middle East are rearranging to meet the conditions that must exist when Antichrist makes his appearance. All these prophecies about what will happen in the Middle East when Antichrist takes over this richest part of the world in oil and natural resources may not be exactly clear at this time; but we see conditions being brought about to make their fulfillment possible.

This will be the most terrible war and time of bloodshed the world has ever seen as three great confederacies meet on the plains of Palestine for the last world war. As it was in days of old when the Assyrian, Babylonian, Persian, Grecian, Egyptian, and Syrian armies squashed little Israel between them in combat, it will happen again on an even greater scale. Israel will suffer as never before in all her tragic history. It is no wonder that this time is called "the time of Jacob's troubles."

We read the last two verses of Daniel chapter eleven: *"But tidings out of the east and out of the north shall trouble him: therefore he shall go forth with great fury to destroy, and utterly to make away many. And he shall plant the tabernacles of his palace between the seas in the glorious holy mountain; yet he shall come to his end, and none shall help him."* As we look to the north of Israel today, we see two great powers rising up — the Common Market of Europe and the powerful communist nation of Russia. Russia will suffer a great defeat when its forces march across the mountains of Israel as described in Ezekiel chapter thirty-eight. But it is evident that at the end of the tribulation, Russia will regather its armed forces and plan to march with communist China against the Antichrist. This is the only possible explanation at this time of verse forty-four. In Revelation 16:12 we are told that the Euphrates River would be dried up so that a great army from the east can be marched across it en route to Israel. Today China is rapidly becoming a nation to be reckoned with. For the past thousand years, China has been a weak and impoverished nation, but here at the end of the age it has risen up with the other nations to take its place in the pavilion of prophecy. And we are told here in Daniel 11:44 that another great and terrible battle will occur when this great army out of the north and the east will come against the Antichrist

We read in Zechariah 14:1-3: *"Behold, the day of the Lord cometh, and thy spoil shall be divided in the midst of thee. For I will gather all nations against Jerusalem to battle; and the city shall be taken, and the houses rifled . . . Then the Lord go forth, and fight against those nations, as when he fought in the day of battle."*

The Lord assured Daniel that even though the nation of Israel would be downtrodden by the Gentiles to the time of the end, this most wicked and cruel of all the transgressors, the Antichrist, would come to an untimely end. And even though he will be successful in planting his own tabernacles — his own churches and seats of authority — in Jerusalem, God will not permit them to desecrate the land of Israel for long. They will all be destroyed by the brightness of His coming. All the military might of the Antichrist will be obliterated from the face of the earth and he, along with the strange god he has consorted with, the false prophet, will be cast into the lake of fire. We read of this great event in Revelation 19:19-20: *"And I saw the beast, and the kings of the earth, and their armies, gathered together to make war against him that sat on the horse, and against his army. And the beast was taken, and with him the false prophet that wrought miracles before him, with which he deceived them that had received the mark of the beast, and them that worshipped his image. These both were cast alive into a lake of fire burning with brimstone."*

The Lord explained to Daniel that the destruction

of this last world ruler, the willful king, also called the Antichrist, would end the desecration of Israel and the holy places by the Gentiles. No other nation of the earth has suffered like Israel. It has been a continual battleground. After the Romans destroyed the city in 70 A.D., the Jews lived in the nations of the world, without a national homeland. Yet in spite of the fact that they have been without a country for almost two thousand years, God has brought them back and established them again in their own land. But even so, according to the prophecies, their troubles are not over because their great trial lies just ahead. The Jew is a witness to God's Word that He has a plan and purpose for this world. This plan and purpose concerns a kingdom of nations over which the Lord Jesus Christ will reign. The Jew back in the land today is the greatest sign of our time that Jesus is coming soon.

Chapter Twelve

In the last verse of chapter eleven, Daniel is informed that the Antichrist would plant the tabernacle of his palace between the seas in the glorious holy mountain. This is an overall explanation of the abomination of desolation, and it will occur at the midway point of the tribulation. Let us continue and read Daniel 12:1: *"And at that time shall Michael stand up, the great prince which standeth for the children of thy people: and there shall be a time of trouble, such as never was since there was a nation even to that same time: and at that time thy people shall be delivered, every one that shall be found written in the book."*

At the beginning of this verse, the Lord says: *". . . at that time shall Michael stand up, the great prince which standeth for the children of thy people. . . ."* To what particular time is the Lord referring? To the time when Antichrist will plant his tabernacle, his church, on Mount Zion, the one spot in all the earth that God has reserved for the throne of His only begotten Son, Jesus Christ. When this happens, and Antichrist stands on this holy spot declaring himself to be God, Michael, the archangel, is going to stand up. In Daniel 10:21, Michael is declared to be the prince of Daniel, meaning of course, the prince of Israel. And here in verse one of chapter twelve he is again set forth as the guardian of Israel.

At the time the Antichrist commits the abomination of desolation, he receives the deadly wound. Then Antichrist turns on Israel, and in accordance with the instructions of Jesus in the Olivet Discourse, the Jews flee toward Petra for their lives. It is then that Michael will stand up for Israel. The course of events is described in more detail in Revelation 12:6-9: *"And the woman* [Israel] *fled into the wilderness, where she hath a place prepared of God, that they should feed her there a thousand two hundred and threescore days. And there was war in heaven: Michael and his angels fought against the dragon; and the dragon fought and his angels, And prevailed not; neither was their place found any more in heaven. And the great dragon was cast out, that old serpent, called the Devil, and Satan, which deceiveth the whole world: he was cast out into the earth, and his angels were cast out with him."*

Reading the corresponding reference in Daniel with Revelation 12:6 shows plainly that the woman is not the Virgin Mary nor the church, but rather, Israel. When Michael and his army of angels go to help Israel, the devil and all his angels stand in the way to prevent it. It is then that the battle that began when Lucifer, the bright and shining one, who left his estate to oppose God, will be finally joined. The issue can be delayed no longer — one must be the ultimate victor and one must be the final loser. Those who worship the devil in Satan's churches believe that the devil will win this war, but the Bible says that God's forces under the leadership of Michael will win it.

Michael's army will rout the army of Satan and he and all his fallen angels will be cast out of the heavens unto the earth. Exactly what the casting out of Satan and his angels out of the heavens into the earth means is difficult to comprehend. The reason it is difficult to understand is because angels are spirit beings. If our own Air Force were to force a squadron of Russian planes flying over the United States territory to either land or shoot them down to the ground, this we could readily understand. But this relatively simple illustration may not be as unrelated to what will actually happen as we might think. From Ezekiel 28:18 it is evident that the devil and his angels hold strong and well-fortified sanctuaries in outer space, and celestial transportation machines are connected with angelic travel through space. Once the devil is cast down to earth, he will enter into the body of Antichrist and the man of sin will become Satan incarnate. In conjunction with this event, let us consider Isaiah chapter fourteen: *"How art thou fallen from heaven, O Lucifer, son of the morning! how art thou cut down to the ground, which didst weaken the nations!"* (Isa. 14:12). This refers prophetically to the casting of Satan and his angels out of the heavens down to the earth by Michael. *"For thou hast said in thine heart, I will ascend into heaven,*

I will exalt my throne above the stars of God: I will sit also upon the mount of the congregation, in the sides of the north: I will ascend above the heights of the clouds; I will be like the most High" (Isa. 14:13-14). These two verses describe Satan's ambition from the very beginning of his rebellion against God's sovereign authority. During the tribulation, he will make his supreme effort to take over the universe and rule over God. Satan worshippers today believe that he will succeed. *"Yet thou shalt be brought down to hell, to the sides of the pit. They that see thee shall narrowly look upon thee, and consider thee, saying, Is this the man that made the earth to tremble, that did shake kingdoms"* (Isa. 14:15-16). This scene describes Satan's estate as he takes the form of man, and those who have been deceived by him and worshipped him as their god consider his fallen and lowly condition. Nevertheless, he will not be robbed of all his power. Like a wounded snake, he will still be dangerous and vengeful. We read in Revelation 12:12: *"Therefore rejoice, ye heavens, and ye that dwell in them. Woe to the inhabiters of the earth and of the sea! for the devil is come down unto you, having great wrath, because he knoweth that he hath but a short time."* We read the corresponding warning given in Daniel 12:1: *". . . and there shall be a time of trouble, such as never was since there was a nation even to that same time. . . ."* And Jesus said of this last three and a half years of the tribulation in Matthew 24:21: *"For then shall be great tribulation, such as was not since the beginning of the world to this time, no, nor ever shall be.*"

The first to feel the great wrath of Satan will be Israel, as we read in Daniel 12:1: "*. . . and at that time thy people shall be delivered, every one that shall be found written in the book.*" It is evident that not all of the Jews will escape. Only those who have come to the knowledge of the truth that Jesus Christ is the true Messiah. We read in Zechariah 14:2: "*. . . and half of the city shall go forth into captivity, and the residue of the people shall not be cut off from the city.*" Of course, this could mean that approximately half of the Jews will accept the Antichrist as their messiah, and these will have nothing to fear. It could also refer to the geographic division of the Jerusalem of today. The old part of Jerusalem remained in Jordan after 1948, and the Jews built a new Jerusalem adjacent to the old Jerusalem on the Israeli side. Both explanations could apply, and this could mean that Jordan will get back the old Jerusalem when the Antichrist confirms the covenant.

We continue and read Daniel 12:2: "*And many of them that sleep in the dust of the earth shall awake, some to everlasting life, and some to shame and everlasting contempt.*"

The setting for verse two is still in the tribulation. The resurrection of the church is not in view here, because the rapture of the church will have already occurred. There is no evidence that the church will go through the tribulation. Every saved person of the dispensation of grace will be resurrected before the tribulation begins. Daniel was not concerned about the Gentiles; he was concerned only about his people. The resurrection described by the Lord in this scripture relates only to Israel. It in no way teaches a general resurrection. Some of Israel will be raised to everlasting life, and some of Israel will be raised to everlasting shame and contempt.

The resurrection of the redeemed of Israel is always associated with the appearance of the Messiah to bring in the kingdom. Israel's impotent plight back in their own land, their flight into the wilderness from Antichrist, the coming of the Lord, and the resurrection of the righteous are put in proper perspective in Isaiah 26:18-21: *"We have been with child, we have been in pain, we have as it were brought forth wind; we have not wrought any deliverance in the earth; neither have the inhabitants of the world fallen. Thy dead men shall live, together with my dead body shall they arise. Awake and sing, ye that dwell in dust: for thy dew is as the dew of herbs, and the earth shall cast out the dead. Come, my people, enter thou into thy chambers, and shut thy doors about thee: hide thyself as it were for a little moment, until the indignation be overpast. For, behold, the Lord cometh out of his place to punish the inhabitants of the earth for their iniquity. . . ."*

Some believe that both the saved and lost of Israel will be raised at this time; however, this would appear to be in contradiction to Revelation 20:5-6: *"But the rest of the dead lived not again until the thousand years were finished. This is the first resurrec-*

tion. Blessed and holy is he that hath part in the first resurrection: on such the second death hath no power. . . ." Certainly, all those Jews who continue in their rebellious ways will be gathered out of the nations and suffer perdition when the Lord comes back. Matthew 13:41-42 refers to their fate: *"The Son of man shall send forth his angels, and they shall gather out of his kingdom all things that offend, and them which do iniquity; And shall cast them into a furnace of fire: there shall be wailing and gnashing of teeth."* Some contend that the resurrection of Daniel 12:2 pertains only to a spiritual resurrection of Israel, but we believe there are too many scriptures connecting the hope of resurrection of redeemed Israel to the coming of the Lord to believe that it relates only to a spiritual rebirth. Certainly, there will be a spiritual rebirth of Israel at this time, but there will also be a literal resurrection.

We continue and read Daniel 12:3: *"And they that be wise shall shine as the brightness of the firmament; and they that turn many to righteousness as the stars for ever and ever."*

This wonderful promise has often been applied to soul-winning Christians, and it does apply to them indirectly, because all who win souls to Jesus Christ are wise and they will receive the most cherished of all rewards. However, this promise is made directly to those who wins souls during the tribulation, and particularly to the 144,000 witnesses of God. We read in Revelation 7:1-8 that twelve thousand out of each of the twelve tribes of Israel will be called to be soul winners during the tribulation. Their ministry will be the most difficult of all of God's servants who preceded them. They will witness children dying by the thousands of famine; they will witness sin and abominations on earth the likes of which men have never committed; and they will witness millions beheaded by the guillotine because they refuse to worship the beast and receive his mark. Yet they will go throughout the world testifying that Jesus is the Christ and calling sinners to have their sins washed in His blood. We read of their converts in Revelation 7:9-17, and we read in verse fourteen: "*. . . These are they which came out of great tribulation, and have washed their robes, and made them white in the blood of the Lamb.*"

Dr. Louis Talbot in his commentary on Daniel told of the power of the witness of a born-again Jew. A young man in Paris, Texas, after he entered the ministry, visited a woman who had been paralyzed for many years with painful arthritis. He did his best to explain the way of salvation to her, but she and her mother invited him to leave. He returned to his church and sadly explained the experience to his co-pastor, a Hebrew Christian by the name of Joseph Flacks. Rev. Flacks quietly put on his hat and left. The next Sunday Dr. Talbot was surprised to see this woman entering church in a wheelchair pushed by her mother, and both were smiling and joyfulling telling everyone that they had accepted Christ as their Savior When he inquired as to how it happened, they explained that Rev. Flacks had visited them, and as he held the sick woman's hand, tears ran down his face as he prayed that God would put her affliction upon him and let the woman walk. The difference was that the Hebrew brother had a deeper compassion for souls; this explains why the 144,000 will win so many souls during the great tribulation.

If Christians today had this kind of compassion for lost souls, we could convert the world. No wonder it is said of soul-winners during the tribulation, that they will shine *". . . as the stars for ever and ever."*

As we finish our study of the book of Daniel, we continue with Daniel 12:4: *"But thou, O Daniel, shut up the words, and seal the book, even to the time of the end: many shall run to and fro, and knowledge shall be increased."*

There is a difference of opinion among Bible scholars as to what the Lord meant when He told Daniel to shut up the words and seal the book. Some even contend that the entire book is sealed to the time of the end, and it should not be taught at all during the dispensation of grace. However, Jesus did not consider it a sealed book and He referred to a portion of Daniel's prophecy in the Olivet Discourse. The Jewish historian Josephus had no difficulty in interpreting the prophecies of Daniel which had been fulfilled up to the time of the destruction of the temple in 70 A.D. Therefore, when our Lord instructed Daniel to seal up the book to the time of the end, it is evident that He did not mean that we should not study it today, or that no one could understand it until the last half of the tribulation. Modern Jewish scholars divide Daniel into two books. One school of thought divides it into two portions according to language. The part that was written in Hebrew is considered one book, and the part that was written in Aramaic is considered a second book. Others divide the book according to subject matter. Chapters one through six are put in one book because they are of a historical nature, and chapters seven through twelve are assembled in a second book because they are apocalyptic. But Josephus divided Daniel into several books. The reason for the divisions set forth by the historian is because the original text was recorded on scrolls, and each division was bound together as a separate set of scrolls. Chapters ten, eleven, and twelve constitute one division because they deal with a single prophetic episode. Therefore, the command to seal the book to the time of the end might possibly be restricted to the last three chapters. We introduce this thought only as a suggestion. Certainly, there are definite prophecies in chapter eleven that no one will be able to understand completely until the last half of the tribulation. In any event, it is evident that during the tribulation the Jews will be searching the Scriptures, and especially the prophecies of Daniel.

In verse four we are given to understand that at the time of the end many would run to and fro and knowledge would be increased. As we behold the communications and transportation networks of our day we do indeed see people running to and fro. From the time of Daniel to 1850, a period of almost twenty-five hundred years, there probably would not have been over a few days difference at most in the time it would take to travel from Europe to the United States. The ships in Daniel's day traveled almost as fast as the ships in the early 1800s. Then about the middle of the nineteenth century steamships began to appear, trains began to replace stagecoaches, and then came the airplane. People are certainly running to and fro.

Also, knowledge has increased. Every parent feels that their children must get an education; they must go to school and get a degree. Some say that man's knowledge today is doubling every two and a half years. Education is not only booming in our nation, but in all the nations of Africa, Asia, and South America where just a few years ago less than five percent of the population could either read or write. This prophecy gives irrefutable proof that we are rapidly approaching the time of the end — the time of the tribulation.

We agree with those who believe the prophecy concerning the increase of knowledge has a double meaning. It also refers to an increase of knowledge relating to the prophecies given in Daniel.

We continue by reading Daniel 12:5-7: *"Then I Daniel looked, and, behold, there stood other two, the one on this side of the bank of the river, and the other on that side of the bank of the river. And one said to the man clothed in linen, which was upon the waters of the river, How long shall it be to the end of these wonders? And I heard the man clothed in linen, which was upon the waters of the river, when he held up his right hand and his left hand unto heaven, and sware by him that liveth for ever that it shall be for a time, times, and an half; and when he shall have accomplished to scatter the power of the holy people, all these things shall be finished."*

The man clothed in linen is Jesus Christ, the One who gave Daniel the prophecy of what would come upon his people before the Messiah would come to bring in the kingdom and fulfill the covenant. The two men on either side of the river are the two witnesses, Moses and Elijah. On the Mount of Transfiguration Jesus explained to Moses and Elijah why the kingdom would not be brought in at that time, and He told them that their ministry to the world would be delayed for a dispensation. They asked the Lord in the vision given to Daniel how long it would take for the prophecies concerning the time of trouble referred to in verse one of the twelfth chapter to be fulfilled. And the reply the Lord gave was as much for their benefit as Daniel, because they must testify in Jerusalem during this entire period. We read the account of their ministry during the last three and a half years of the tribulation in Revelation chapter eleven. The scene which Daniel saw here in the twelfth chapter is repeated again in Revelation 10:1-7: *"And I saw*

*another mighty angel come down from heaven,
clothed with a cloud: and a rainbow was upon his
head, and his face was as it were the sun, and his feet as
pillars of fire: And he had in his hand a little book
open: and he set his right foot upon the sea, and his left
foot on the earth . . . And the angel which I saw stand
upon the sea and upon the earth lifted up his hand to
heaven, And sware by him that liveth for ever and
ever . . . that there should be time no longer . . . the
mystery of God should be finished, as he hath
declared to his servants the prophets."*

The reference by the Lord in the tenth chapter of
Revelation to time means the beginning of those
things prophesied for the last half of the tribulation as
He informed the prophets, among whom Daniel is
perhaps the principal one. In the eleventh chapter of
Revelation the two witnesses appear to bring to pass
those things prophesied concerning judgment upon
the Antichrist and his kingdom. But the two witnesses
are informed in Daniel 12:7 that from the time the
willful king of the eleventh chapter of Daniel, the
Antichrist, begins to scatter Israel and they flee for
their lives, it will be three and a half years before the
time of Jacob's troubles will be brought to an end.

We continue and read Daniel 12:8-9: *"And I
heard, but I understood not: then said I, O my Lord,
what shall be the end of these things? And he said, Go
thy way, Daniel: for the words are closed up and
sealed till the time of the end."*

At the beginning of the prophecy Daniel begged

to be excused from further revelations, because he was terrified at those things which would come upon his nation. But at the conclusion of the revelation, he begged to be shown more. His understanding was not complete and he wanted to be shown how the Lord would come and destroy the Antichrist and bring in the kingdom. And in response, Jesus Christ kindly informed Daniel that he had seen enough, to just write his words down because their meaning would not be fully understood until the time of the end. The reply which the Lord gave Daniel indicates further that the portion of Daniel which is to be especially sealed until the time of the end are the prophecies dealing with the last three and a half years of the tribulation.

We continue and read Daniel 12:10-11: *"Many shall be purified, and made white, and tried; but the wicked shall do wickedly: and none of the wicked shall understand; but the wise shall understand. And from the time that the daily sacrifice shall be taken away, and the abomination that maketh desolate set up, there shall be a thousand two hundred and ninety days."*

The subject of these two verses remains the same: the end of Israel's troubles in the time of great tribulation. Concerning the specific days of the great tribulation, we read in Revelation 11:3 that the ministry of the two witnesses in Jerusalem will last for twelve hundred sixty days. We also read in Revelation 12:6 that Israel will be hid from the Antichrist in the wilderness for the same time period. These two time periods agree perfectly with the Lord's instructions to the two witnesses in Daniel 12:7, because he told them that their ministry would begin at the time that the Antichrist began to scatter the Jews, and their ministry would continue during the absence of Israel from the land. Therefore, the length of their ministry coincides with the time that Israel will be hid from the wrath of Antichrist. We come to Daniel 12:11 where we are informed that from the time Antichrist stands in the temple and declares himself to be God, to the restoration of Israel to the land would be twelve hundred ninety days — an extra month, or thirty days. Although we do not know for sure, we assume an extra thirty days will be required to regather the Jews. The angels are to go into all the nations of the world and bring back all the twelve tribes to Palestine. There will not be an Israelite left in any Gentile nation. We read in Mark 13:26-27: *"And then shall they see the Son of man coming in the clouds with great power and glory. And then shall he send his angels, and shall gather together his elect from the four winds, from the uttermost part of the earth to the uttermost part of heaven."* And we read in other scriptures that the Lord will bring them back from all nations. In verse ten is it indicated that regardless of their spiritual states, both righteous and wicked will be gathered back into the land.

We read Daniel 12:12-13: *"Blessed is he that waiteth, and cometh to the thousand three hundred and five and thirty days. But go thou thy way till the end be: for thou shalt rest, and stand in thy lot at the end of the days."*

In verse ten it is indicated that when the Lord comes Israel will be tried. We read this also in Zechariah 13:8-9: *"And it shall come to pass, that in all the land, saith the Lord, two parts therein shall be cut off and die; but the third shall be left therein. And I will bring the third part through the fire, and will refine them as silver is refined, and will try them as gold is tried: they shall call on my name, and I will hear them: I will say, It is my people: and they shall say, the Lord is my God."*

This scripture is to be understood in conjunction with Matthew 13:41-43: *"The Son of man shall send forth his angels, and they shall gather out of his kingdom all things that offend, and them which do iniquity; And shall cast them into a furnace of fire: there shall be wailing and gnashing of teeth. Then shall the righteous shine forth as the sun in the kingdom of their Father. . . ."*

The extra forty-five days will be required for the judgment of Israel and the giving of rewards to the righteous and redeemed. Daniel was assured that at the end of the thirteen hundred thirty-five days, he would stand in his lot, meaning his own place in the kingdom. But many of the wicked will be cast out of the kingdom. According to the promise made to Daniel by the Lord, the prophet has a very special place reserved for him in this glorious reign of Jesus Christ over the earth.

We read in Matthew 13:47-50: *". . . The kingdom of heaven is like unto a net . . . Which, when it was full, they drew to shore . . . and gathered the good into vessels, but cast the bad away. So shall it be at the end of the world* [age]: *the angels shall come forth, and sever the wicked from among the just, And shall cast them into the furnace of fire: there shall be wailing and gnashing of teeth."* This has nothing to do with the church. It has nothing to do with the judgment of the nations. It refers only to the judgment of Israel when Christ returns. It will be then that Jesus Christ will bring in the kingdom of Heaven and those things which Daniel prayed for his people, Israel, will all be fulfilled.

The prophecies of Daniel prove to us today that this age is rapidly drawing to a close and the time of the end is near. Certainly we are living in troublesome times, but for a troubled world, let us give forth the message of 2 Thessalonians 1:7-10: *"And to you who are troubled rest with us, when the Lord Jesus shall be revealed from heaven with his mighty angels, In flaming fire taking vengeance on them that know not God, and that obey not the gospel of our Lord Jesus Christ: Who shall be punished with everlasting destruction from the presence of the Lord, and from the glory of his power; When he shall come to be glorified in his saints, and to be admired in all them that believe. . . ."*

Noah Hutchings is president of The Southwest Radio Church, one of the foremost prophetic ministries in the world. He has written dozens of books and booklets on prophecy and other Bible themes. Pastor Hutchings has been active in missions and communication ministries for 39 years and is recognized for being a world traveller, having led tours to Israel, Iraq, Egypt, Europe, China, and other nations around the world. His plain and conversational style of writing makes the subject matter he approaches both interesting and informative to the reader, regardless of the level of education or understanding.